An Introduct
Challenging Topics For Young Muslims

BOOK 2

By Dr Abdul Qader Ismail

Edited by Dr Musharraf Hussain

Invitation Publishing

First Edition Published February 2021

INVITATION PUBLISHING
512-514 Berridge Road West
Nottingham
NG7 5JU

Distributed by INVITATION PUBLISHING
Tel: +44[0] 115 855 0961
E-mail: info@invitationpublishing.co.uk

Cataloguing-in-Publication Data is available from the British Library.

ISBN: 978-1902248912

For my mother and the mother of my children - our first, and most important teachers.

Written by Dr Abdul Qader Ismail BMBCh (Oxon), MA (Oxon), MRCPCH, under the spiritual guidance of Khwaja Muhammad Ulfat Qadri Naqshbandi (Lahore, Pakistan), and Pir Mohammad Tayyab Ur-Rahman Qadri (Qadria Trust, UK; Bhera Shareef, Haripur, Pakistan).

My most heartfelt thanks to Mullah Adil Bader, Dr Syed Mutaheer Ali, and Mrs Atheah Gsouma for their help in writing, editing and proofreading this book. These individuals consented for their inclusion in this acknowledgement, however, this does not mean they agree entirely with all, or any, of what is written in this book. Similarly, I have not acted upon all their feedback and suggestions during the writing, editing and proofreading process.

I would also like to thank Mr Atif Hussain for keeping me involved during the editing and publishing process, and Dr Musharraf Hussain for his continued encouragement and support.

Contents

Foreword

Young people are at a critical stage between childhood and adulthood. They are thinking on a higher level than children, but not yet confident in their view of the world like adults. Whilst children think logically about the concrete, the here and now, young people can think in abstract terms, about God, the life Hereafter and global concepts like the climate crisis. They have a heightened sense of justice, politics and patriotism. If they are not guided, they can develop unIslamic views on these topics and even accept conspiracy theories and extremist views. That is why it is so important that we guide young people. Dr Abdul Qader Ismail is to be congratulated on writing 'An Introduction to Challenging Topics for Young Muslims'. This book is a comprehensive manual for young people. He tackles subjects from belief in Allah to blood donation; from Riba to racism; and gambling to gender. He has based his book entirely on teachings of the Quran and the Sunnah of the blessed Messenger (peace be upon him). He has been thorough in ensuring that these sensitive matters are presented in a logical and effective style.

As young people wrestle with socio-religious, moral and spiritual perspectives it is important to provide them clear guidelines, set boundaries of dos and don'ts; give them confidence that they are special and they have not been left alone to wonder in the wilderness of a largely secular and sometimes aggressively atheist society. Nor are they left at the mercy of social media platforms to inform themselves of such important issues.

Dr Abdul Qader Ismail is a young paediatrician trained at Oxford University. His passion to educate his family and the Muslim youth is to be much-admired. I pray Allah give him more energy, time and resources to continue doing this kind of educational work.

Dr Musharraf Hussain Al-Azhari

(Translator of 'The Majestic Quran')

Introduction

The topics introduced in this book include:

- Philosophical and theological questions, such as why do we believe in God, why there are so many different religions, why there are so many sects in Islam?
- Some common objections raised against Islam, e.g. validity of the Qur'an and Hadith, apparent contradictions between Islam and science, and Hudud punishments in the Shariah.
- Current issues regarding relationships and gender identity, vegetarianism and environmentalism.
- Behavioural, physical and mental health issues, e.g. coping with the stress of exams, obesity, anxiety and depression, self-harm and suicide.
- Addictive habits e.g. drugs, alcohol and smoking, gambling, and watching pornography.

These are all important socioreligious topics which are introduced in school, by friends, or on the internet. The information we gain from these sources may not be accurate, will very likely be secular, or worse, have an Islamophobic agenda. This can have very damaging consequences; it can create serious doubt in our minds regarding our faith especially when we have not yet developed a strong, personal relationship with it.

Parents and Islamic school teachers should be involved when using this book as a guide to navigate these topics so that you can develop a strong foundation and a firm understanding of your faith. You will realise how Allah and His Prophet (peace be upon him), in the Qur'an and Hadith, and through the interpretation of Islamic scholars in every age, have provided us with important principles and guidance which are as relevant today as they were over 1400 years ago. This is an ongoing process as the world, society and science evolve, so too does our understanding of our faith. This will better prepare you for the secular and sometimes hostile environment encountered in schools, in the media and on the internet.

2. RACE, GENDER AND RELATIONSHIPS IN ISLAM

2.1

Racism

Objectives

- To understand the wisdom behind Allah creating us of different races
- To explore why racism is incompatible with the Islamic faith
- To consider the impact of racism on the perpetrator and the victim

Keywords

- Racism
- Arrogance
- Superiority
- Oppression

What is 'race'?

Human beings from different parts of the world have different coloured skin and different facial features. For example, people from Africa can have very dark skin (called black, even though it is really dark brown), and in some parts of Africa, wide noses, full lips and very curly hair, almost like wool. People from parts of Asia can be shorter and smaller, they have slightly yellow coloured skin, and their eyes look thinner because their eyelids cover more of their eyes. People from parts of Europe can have pale white skin, blue eyes, blond hair, and thin noses and lips.

Historically, these differences have been used to divide people into races (such as Caucasian or white, Afro-Carribean or black, Asian, etc.), and it was believed these differences were not just to do with skin colour and facial features, but also personality and behaviour (such as intelligence and violence). However, with modern advances in genetics, biologists tell us that all humans share 99.9% of their DNA (the genetic instructions contained within each of the roughly 30 trillion cells within our bodies, that tell our bodies how to grow and function). This means we cannot use race to make generalisations about people, just because someone is of a certain race that doesn't tell us how clever they are, or friendly, or likely to commit violence, or anything else about them, except maybe to give us a rough idea of the colour of their skin and how they will look.

What is racism?

Racism is the belief that one race is better or worse than another. A racist person believes that race makes a difference to what kind of person you are, and that it is justified to have prejudices against, or persecute people of a different race (such as white people enslaving black people).

The first act of racism

When Allah created the Prophet Adam's body (peace be upon him) from clay and blew his soul into him, all the Angels were instructed to bow down to him. Iblis (Shaitan) was a Jinn who was allowed to live with the Angels as a reward for his millennia of worship.

Remember when Your Lord said to Angels, "I am creating a human with dried clay from dark mud. Once I have shaped and blown My spirit into him, then prostrate before him." So all the Angels prostrated, except Iblis, who refused to prostrate. (Qur'an 15:28-31)

"What stopped you from prostrating when I commanded you?" said Allah, he (Iblis) replied, "I am better than him since You created me from fire, and him from clay." (Qur'an 7:12)

So it could be argued that the first act of racism was that of Iblis, and it was this that stopped him from obeying Allah.

Celebrating our differences in Islam

Islam actively discourages racism. Allah repeatedly tells us in the Qur'an how tremendous His creation is, and how He made people of different colours and speaking different languages.

Another of His signs is the creation of the Heavens and the Earth, and the differences in your languages and skin colour, there are signs for those who know. (Qur'an 30:22)

He talks about how the Earth is of different colours, white, red and black, and how He also made animals and people of different colours.

Haven't you considered, how Allah sends rain from the sky, that produces fruits of different colours; look at the mountains with streaks of white and red rock of various shades, some pitch black? In the same way, colour differences exist among people and wild and domesticated animals... (Qur'an 35:27-28)

Allah tells us He made people in different nations and tribes, in different races, so we can get to know each other.

People, We created you from a male and female; then made you into different races and tribes so you may know each other... (Qur'an 49:13)

The Prophet (peace be upon him) told us that an Arab is not better than a non-Arab, and a non-Arab is not better than an Arab, white is not better than black, and black is not better than white.

The Prophet (peace be upon him) said: "O people, verily your Lord is One and your father is one. Verily there is no superiority of an Arab over a non-Arab or of a non-Arab over an Arab, or of a red man over a black man, or of a black man over a red man, except in terms of Taqwa (God consciousness, or piety). (Al Albani)

The companions of the Prophet (may Allah be pleased with them all)

The Prophet (peace be upon him) had followers who were from different countries, of different skin colours and who spoke different languages. He never treated them any differently based on any of these things, and he did not allow his followers to treat each other differently either.

Syedina Bilal was black; he was a slave until Syedina Abu-Bakr (may Allah be pleased with them both) freed him. Syedina Abu-Bakr used to call Bilal his master (may Allah be pleased with them both) and the Prophet (peace be upon him)

made Bilal the Muezzin (the person who gives the Adhan). When the Muslims conquered Makkah, the Prophet (peace be upon him) told Bilal to stand on the roof the Ka'bah and give the Adhan.

Syedina Salman al-Farsi (may Allah be pleased with him) was from Persia (modern day Iran), and he arrived in Madinah as a slave. However, the Prophet (peace be upon him) loved him so much he said that Salman was one of his family. At the battle of Tabuk, Syedina Salman al-Farsi (may Allah be pleased with him) suggested digging a trench around Madinah to protect them from the huge enemy army, and this is what the Muslims did.

Superiority based on race or deeds?

We all came from the Prophet Adam (peace be upon him) if we trace our ancestry back far enough. Just because someone's family is from one country, how does that make them better than someone else, whose family is from another country? Thinking you are better than someone else looking down on, or persecuting them is one of the main reasons why people hurt and even kill other people, and it is why many wars have been fought in the past and continue to be waged today.

As per the Qur'an and the Hadith stated above, Allah and His Prophet (peace be upon him) have told us that the only thing which makes one person better than another is their piety.

... Indeed, the most honourable in the sight of Allah is the most mindful of Allah, the Knower, the Aware. (Qur'an 49:13)

Allah does not care what language we speak, which country we come from, the colour of our skin, whether we are beautiful or ugly, how tall or short we are, how strong we are or how well we can fight, how educated we are or how much money or power we have – none of this matters. And because only Allah knows how pious someone is, we should never think we are better than someone else (even if they are a non-Muslim, or openly commit sins), and we should definitely never persecute someone because we think we are better than they are.

The punishment for racism

When we hurt someone, emotionally or physically, this is called oppression and we are being a tyrant. Allah tells us how He will destroy these people, how they will not be successful and He will throw them into Hell.

Such is the Final Abode; We grant it to those who desire neither grandeur nor wreak havoc in the land. And the best outcome is for those mindful of Allah. Whoever produces good deeds will be rewarded with something wonderful; and whoever produces evil deeds will be rewarded for what they did. (Qur'an 28:83-84)

Anyone who defends himself against injustice mustn't be blamed; the blame is on those who commit injustice and oppress people in the city. For them will be a painful punishment. (Qur'an 42:41-42)

The Prophet (peace be upon him) said, "Allah Almighty said: 'O my servants, I have forbidden injustice for myself and I have forbidden it among you, so do not oppress one another...'" (Muslim)

The Prophet (peace be upon him) also told us that Allah will always accept the prayer of the oppressed, so we should be very careful of not oppressing people since they are likely to curse us.

The Prophet (peace be upon him) said, "Beware of the supplication of the oppressed, for there is no barrier between it and Allah." (Bukhari)

If we have been racist and hurt someone, even if we ask for forgiveness from Allah (do Istighfar), He will not forgive us until we ask for forgiveness from the person we hurt. If we do not ask the people we hurt for forgiveness before we die, then on the Day of Judgement when our good deeds are weighed on the scales, those good deeds will be given in compensation to all the people we have hurt. If our good deeds run out and there are still people left to compensate for our oppression of them, their sins will be given to us. In this way, even if we have spent our whole life worshipping Allah, if we behaved as a tyrant, on the Day of Judgement we could still be led to Hell.

The Prophet (peace be upon him) said: "Do you know who is the bankrupt one?" The people said: 'The bankrupt among us is the one who has neither money nor property.' He (peace be upon him) said: "The real bankrupt one of my nation would be he who would come on the Day of Resurrection having (performed) prayers, (observed) fasting and (spent in) charity, (but he will find himself bankrupt on that Day due to depleting these good deeds) because he despised others, uttered slanderous terms against others,

others, unlawfully devoured the wealth of others, shed the blood of others, and beat others. Therefore, his good deeds would be credited to the account of those (who suffered at his hand). If his good deeds are exhausted, their sins (i.e. those he oppressed) will be entered in his account and he will be thrown into the (Hell) Fire." (Muslim)

When we act in a racist way, we are being proud. We are treating someone else in a bad way because we think we are better than they are. This is a hateful sin in the eyes of Allah, He is the only One with the right to be proud, as per one of His names, Al-Mutakabbir (The Proud), and the Hadith Kudsi:

Allah, the Almighty, says: "Pride is My garment and haughtiness My Mantle: whoever vies with Me for them I will throw into Hell." (Muslim)

It is the sin of Iblis, he was proud and thought he was better than the Prophet Adam (peace be upon and so disobeyed Allah and did not bow down. The Prophet (peace be upon him) told us Allah will not allow anyone to enter Paradise who has even the smallest amount of pride or arrogance in their heart. Furthermore, in the Qur'an Allah has described Hell as being the abode of the proud.

The Prophet (peace be upon him) said: "No one who has an atom's-weight of arrogance in his heart will enter Paradise." A man said, "O Messenger of Allah, what if a man likes his clothes and his shoes to look good?" He said, "Allah is Beautiful and loves beauty. Arrogance means rejecting the truth and looking down on people." (Muslim)

Don't look down on people or swagger about. Allah dislikes every rude boaster. (Qur'an 31:18)

You will see on Judgement Day those who denied Allah, their faces darkened – isn't Hell the final home for the arrogant? (Qur'an 39:60)

Conclusion

It is a blessing of Allah that He has made us of different tribes and nations, so we can learn from each other about our different cultures and languages. How boring would it be if everyone looked, sounded and behaved the same? Racism (persecuting someone of a different race because we believe we are better than them) is against what Allah and His Prophet (peace be upon him) have taught us. In fact, if we do this we are following the example of Shaitan, and like him we will end up in Hell.

Questions

- What is your race?
- Do you have any friends of a different race?
- What is racism?
- Is racism allowed in Islam?
- When we are racist, how are we following the example of Shaitan?

Activities

- Watch documentaries of people who come from different parts of the world to see what they look like and learn about their language and culture
- Talk to your parents/ grandparents about where they came from, and where their ancestors came from
- If you see someone being bullied because of their race, stand up for them

2.2

Gender Issues

Objectives

- To understand the similarities and differences between men and women from the Islamic perspective
- To explore the contribution of women in Islamic history
- To consider what defines gender

Keywords

- Gender
- Male
- Female
- Transsexual

Allah is neither male nor female

Allah is neither male nor female. In translations of the Qur'an the pronoun 'He' is used for Allah, but that is not because He is male. In Arabic the only pronouns are 'he' and 'she', there is no 'it' (like in English), and everything is 'He' unless it is feminine or female. So if we were to translate the Arabic word 'Huwa' as 'She' we would be saying Allah is female, which is wrong. We don't translate 'Huwa' as 'it' because that would be disrespectful. So 'Huwa' is translated as 'He' but this does not mean Allah is male.

In fact, we can see attributes of Allah in both men and women, some stronger in men, some stronger in women. For example, Allah is Rahman and Rahim, meaning the One who protects and loves, who is full of mercy and kindness. These names are where the Arabic word for womb comes from. This tells us how the protection, kindness and love Allah shows to His creation is similar to the protection, kindness and love Allah put in a mother for her children. This does not mean a man cannot be kind to his children, but this attribute is stronger within women. This is the same for names such as Muqit (The Nourisher), Wadud (The Loving), Ghaffar (The Ever Forgiving), and Muhyi (The Giver of Life). Examples of attributes of Allah that are stronger in men include Muhaymin (The Guardian), Razzaq (The Ever Providing), Waliy (The Protecting Friend), Matin (The Firm), and Mumit (The Taker of Life).

Why are men and women different?

Muslims don't believe men are better, more important, or more valuable than women, or vice versa. We become better by the things we do, how much we help the creation of Allah, how much we follow the example of the Prophet (peace be upon him), how much we worship Allah and try to please Him.

...Indeed, the most honourable in the sight of Allah is the most mindful of Allah, the Knower, the Aware. (Qur'an 49:13)

Men and women who submit to the will of Allah are: believers, devout, truthful, patient, humble, charitable, keep a fast, keep their private parts pure and remember Allah frequently... (Qur'an 33:35)

Allah has however, created the bodies of men and women to be different. The most important difference is that a woman can become pregnant, give birth, and breastfeed her baby. At the same time, a man has to be able to provide food, shelter, and protection for his pregnant wife. In ancient times this meant he had to be quick and strong, able to hunt and fight, and build a shelter. This is reflected in how Allah has designed and created our bodies.

In general, men are taller, heavier, faster, stronger than women,

although that does not mean some women are not bigger and stronger than some men. Women develop faster than men, from even before they are born (baby girls born prematurely have better survival chances than premature boys), when they are little girls (they develop fine-motor and language skills faster), and going through puberty (the average age is 11 for girls and 12 for boys).

There are also differences in the way they think and the kind of things they like, and this can even be seen in little children. Boys like playing fighting games, and with trucks and action figures, girls like playing games where they are taking care of dolls and cooking (experiments with male and female monkeys displaying similar preferences for the kinds of toys they play with have shown that this is not just due to societal conditioning). But this does not mean some boys do not like playing with dolls, or some girls do not like playing with trucks.

What jobs can men and women do?

Islam does not forbid a woman from doing Halal work outside of the home to support her family, nor a man from staying home, taking care of the children and doing household chores. In fact, the Prophet himself (peace be upon him), used to help his wives with the housework and Allah told us the Prophet (peace be upon him) has the most excellent character and we should copy it.

Syedatuna Aisha (may Allah be pleased with her), the wife of the Prophet Muhammad (peace be upon him), was asked, "What did the Prophet (peace be upon him) used to do in his house?" She replied, "He used to keep himself busy serving his family and when it was the time for prayer he would go for it." (Bukhari)

You have an excellent role model in the Messenger of Allah, particularly for anyone who longs for Allah and the last day and remembers Him abundantly. (Qur'an 33:21)

However, even if a woman works, she does not have to use her money to help support her family. In Islam this is the responsibility of her husband. She can keep her money and use it in whatever Halal ways she wants. This is why, when the Qur'an talks about the inheritance men and women get, women get half as much as men. This is because Allah has not given women the same responsibility to support their families as He has men.

So in general, a woman can do any job that a man can do, Islam does not say she has to be a housewife. But Islam does recognise that perhaps the most important job in the world is raising children, and it is very difficult to do it well. This involves teaching them to excel in whatever they do and make the world a better place, teaching them to be good human beings and Muslims, and teaching them how to get close to Allah and His Prophet (peace be upon him) so they can enter Paradise. Allah has made women better able to do this than men.

How should men and women treat each other in marriage?

Since Allah is the One who created human beings, He knows how they behave. He knows that in a marriage, where a man and woman come together to spend their life with each other, many decisions need to be made and sometimes there will be arguments. In this relationship Islam asks the husband to talk to his wife and ask her advice, and it asks the wife to offer her husband advice and support his decisions. Both of them should always behave with respect towards each other. Both men and women can choose to get divorced if they don't want to stay married to each other, but of all the permissible acts, Allah dislikes divorce the most.

The Prophet's own example (peace be upon him) was that he would spend time with his wives, ask and follow their advice, play games and joke with them, and never get angry or shout at them.

The Prophet (peace be upon him) said, "Any woman who dies while her husband is pleased with her, she will enter Paradise." (Tirmidhi)

Syedina Amr Bin al-As (may Allah be pleased with him) reported that he asked the Prophet (peace be upon him): "O Allah's Messenger! Who is the most beloved to you among the people?" He replied; "Aisha..." (Bukhari)

Syedatuna Aisha (may Allah be pleased with her) said: "I would drink then I would hand it [the vessel] to the Prophet (peace be upon him) and he would put his mouth where mine had been and drink; and I would eat the meat from a bone and he would put his mouth where mine had been." (Muslim)

Syedatuna Safiyyah (one of the Prophet's wives, may Allah be pleased with her) narrated: "The Messenger of Allah (peace be upon him) went to Haj with his wives. On the way my camel knelt down as it was the weakest among all the other camels, and so I wept.

The Prophet came to me and wiped away my tears with his robe and hands..." (Ahmad)

Syedina Anas ibn Malik (may Allah be pleased with him) narrates: "I saw the Prophet (peace be upon him) making for her [Safiyyah] a kind of cushion with his cloak behind him [on his camel]. He then sat beside his camel and put his knee for Safiyyah to put her foot on, in order to ride [on the camel]." (Bukhari)

Syedatuna Aisha (may Allah be pleased with him) reports that the Prophet (peace be upon him) said to her: "Come I will race you." She continues, "So I raced with him and I won. After I became heavier, he raced me and he won, so he laughed and said this one for that one." (Abu Dawood)

The Prophet (peace be upon him) said, "The best of you is the one who is best to his wife, and I am the best of you to my wives." (Tirmidhi)

Worshipping Allah and following His religion

When it comes to worshipping Allah and following the Sunnah (practice) of the Prophet (peace be upon him), there is no difference between men and women. In the Qur'an Allah says:

The believers, both men and women, stand by each other; they enjoin what is good and forbid what is evil; they perform the prayer, pay Zakat, they obey Allah and His Messenger... (Qur'an 9:71)

Both men and women can pray in the Mosque but the Prophet (peace be upon him) told us that for a woman she will get even more reward if she prays in her house.

The Prophet (peace be upon him) said: "Do not prevent your women from going to the mosque, even though their houses are better for them." (Abu Dawood)

A man is never allowed to miss Salah, even if he is fighting a war, even if he cannot stand or sit. If he misses Salah he has to make it up afterwards. But for women Allah has told them that during their period

every month they are allowed to miss the Salah without needing to make up for it afterwards (to give them a rest during this time).

There is no difference between men and women in how close to Allah and His Prophet (peace be upon him) they can get by doing good deeds and refraining from sins. In Islamic history there are many stories of Awliyah Allah that are men and women, and many of the Awliyah Allah who were men talk about women teachers who guided them on their spiritual path.

All of the Prophets were men, but this is because Prophets had to spend their whole lives trying to spread the message of Allah. They had to talk to and meet with people who treated them badly and even tried to hurt or kill them. In olden times people didn't listen to women or didn't think what women had to say was that important. Islam does not teach this, but if a Prophet had been a woman, it would have made her life and her job even harder.

Amazing women in Islam

However, even the Prophets themselves had help from some of the most amazing women. Syedina Adam lived in Paradise with Syedatuna Hawa (peace be upon them both) before they were sent to the Earth.

He created you from a single soul, and from that made its spouse for comfort... (Qur'an 7:189)

Syedatuna Asiyah

The Prophet Musa's life was saved when his own mother put his basket in the river to stop the Pharaoh's soldiers from killing him, and he ended up being taken care of by the wife of the Pharaoh, Syedatuna Asiyah (may Allah be pleased with them all):

We inspired the mother of Musa: "Breastfeed him, but when you fear for him then put him in a basket and let it float on the river, but don't be afraid or sad. We shall return him to you and make him a Messenger. (Qur'an 28:7)

Allah gives an example to the believers of Pharaoh's wife, when she said, "My Lord, build for me a house near You in Paradise, and save me from Pharaoh and his works, and save me from the evildoers." (Qur'an 66:11)

Syedatuna Hajira

The Prophet Ibrahim's wife, Syedatuna Hajira took care of their baby son and future Prophet, Ismail when Allah told him to leave them in the desert. Her running between the hills of Safa and Marwa was so liked by Allah that he made all Muslims copy it during Hajj and Umrah until the Day of Judgement.

...Ibrahim brought her (Hajirah) and her son, Ismail while she was suckling him, to a place near the Ka'bah under a tree on the spot of Zam-Zam, at the highest place in the mosque. During those days there was nobody in Makkah, nor was there any water. So he made them sit over there and placed near them a leather bag containing some dates, and a small water-skin containing some water, and set out homeward. Ismail's mother followed him saying: "O Ibrahim! Where are you going, leaving us in this valley where there is no person whose company we may enjoy, nor is there anything (to enjoy)?" She repeated that to him many times, but he did not look back at her. Then she asked him: "Has Allah ordered you to do so?" He said: "Yes." She said: "Then He will not neglect us," and she returned (to her child) while Ibrahim proceeded on his way. (Bukhari)

The hills of Safa and Marwa are Symbols of Allah; whoever comes to Allah's House to perform the Haj or Umrah, let him know that there is no objection in walking between them... (Qur'an 2:158)

Syedatuna Hannah

Syedatuna Hannah, the mother of Syedatuna Maryam (may Allah be pleased with them both) put her into the care of the Prophet Zachariah (peace be upon him) to spend her life learning about and getting closer to Allah.

When Imran's wife said, "Lord, I vow to dedicate whatever is in my womb to Your service, so accept this vow from me. You are the Hearer, the Knower." When she had given birth to her, she said, "Lord, I gave birth to a girl" – Allah knew well what she had given birth to, the male is not like the female – then she added, "I have named her Maryam, and I place her and her offspring in Your protection from the accursed Satan." Her Lord accepted her and raised her in the best way, and He entrusted her to the care of Zachariah... (Qur'an 3:35-37)

...Whenever Zachariah entered the prayer room, he found fruits next to her; so one day he asked her, "Where do you get this from Maryam?" She replied, "It's from Allah. Indeed, Allah provides boundlessly to whomever He pleases." (Qur'an 3:37)

Syedatuna Maryam

Syedatuna Maryam was blessed by Allah to give birth to the Prophet Isa (peace be upon them both) without a husband, an amazing miracle.

Remember when the Angels said: "Maryam, Allah gives you good news of a Word from Him, his name will be the Messiah, Isa son of Maryam, honoured in this world and in the Hereafter, and among those allowed to approach Allah. He will speak to people from his cradle and as a grown-up, and he will be righteous." She asked, "Lord, how can I have a son when no man has touched me?" The Angel said, "That is how Allah is; He creates whatever He pleases. If He decides something, He simply says, "Be!" and there it is. (Qur'an 3:45-47)

Syedatuna Khadija

The first person to believe in the message of the Prophet Muhammad (peace be upon him) was his wife, Syedatuna Khadija (may Allah be pleased with her). His love for her was so great that even after her death and having married again, he would often remember how she had supported him with everything she had during some of the most difficult times of his life.

Abu Hurayrah (may Allah be pleased with him) narrated that Jibra'il came to the Prophet (peace be upon him) and said: "O Allah's Messenger! This is Khadija coming to you with a dish having meat soup (or some food or drink). When she reaches you, greet her on behalf of her Lord (i.e. Allah) and on my behalf, and give her the glad tidings of having a palace

in Paradise wherein there will be neither any noise nor any fatigue (trouble)." (Bukhari)

The Prophet (peace be upon him) said [regarding Syedatuna Khadija (may Allah be pleased with her)]: "She believed in me when the whole world refuted me and she attested to my trueness when the whole world accused me of falsehood. She offered me compassion and loyalty with her wealth when everyone else had forsaken me." (Ahmad)

Are all children boys or girls?

When some children are born it is not easy to tell if they are a boy or a girl (called intersex). Doctors can do tests and scans of their internal organs to get more information. Sometimes they are boys but they haven't developed normal male genitalia, or they may be girls who have developed so it looks like they have male genitalia (due to abnormal exposure to hormones during pregnancy). Sometimes, as they grow older and go through puberty, due to the release of hormones and further development of their genitalia, it becomes clearer if they are a boy or a girl. But sometimes, if they have been raised as a boy it can be difficult if they later find out they are a girl, or if they have been raised as a girl and they find out they are a boy. They might want to continue being a boy or girl, even if they now find out this does not match their biological gender.

There are medical specialists who care for these children and their families as they go through this difficult time. Medicines and sometimes surgery can help these children behave and have bodies that are male or female. Islam recognises that there are children like this. Allah has made this a test for them and their families, and helping them is a way of pleasing Allah.

Transsexual/ transgender children

There are also some boys or girls whose bodies are normal, but they feel like they should be the opposite gender (called transsexual or transgender). A boy might want to behave like a girl, and a girl might want to behave like a boy. If they take medicine and have surgery, it can make them look like, sound, and behave like the opposite gender.

In Islam this is not allowed. If someone is born as a boy or girl, that is what Allah created them as; they are not allowed to choose to be be the opposite gender. If they have strong feelings to be the opposite gender, that is a test for them. If they pray to Allah to help them and stop themselves from acting upon these feelings, this will please Allah. This also applies to people who have the bodies of men or women but say they are neither male nor female (called agender or genderless).

Conclusion

Allah has created men and women to be different but equally special in their own ways. In some things they are better than each other, in others they are the same. We should always remember that Allah is our Creator, for which part of our gratitude is to live our life in a way that will please Him. However, in the world that we live in there are many people who have the bodies of men or women but want to be, or believe they are something else. Even though as Muslims we believe this goes against the command of Allah, this does not give us permission to look down on or persecute such people. Following the example of the Prophet (peace be upon him), we should love everyone (all of Allah's creation), behave with them as we would want others to treat us, and pray for them.

Questions

- Are men better than women, or are women better than men?
- In what ways are men and women different?
- In what ways are men and women the same?
- Are all children born as boys or girls?
- Are Muslims allowed to change their gender?
- How should we behave with people who are transgender/transsexual/agender?

Activities

- Read a book on the names of Allah, and think about which ones are masculine and which are feminine
- Think of all the special women in your life, and write a list of what makes them so special
- Think of all the special men in your life, and write a list of what makes them so special
- If you see someone being bullied because they are a woman, or transsexual/transgender/agender, stand up for them

2 . 3

Dressing Modestly

Objectives

- To understand why Islam promotes modest dress for both men and women
- To explore the limits and freedoms Islam gives regarding what men and women can wear
- To consider the reasons why people dress immodestly

Keywords

- Clothes
- Covering
- Hijab
- Transvestite

Islam, a complete way of life

Islam is not just a religion but a complete way of life, in that Allah has provided us with instructions regarding every part of our lives. We get these instructions from the Qur'an, and Hadith of the Prophet (peace be upon him). Every commandment or prohibition Allah has placed upon us is done with His infinite wisdom. If we can understand this, it makes it easier to comply and seek Allah's pleasure. However, even if we cannot understand the wisdom behind a certain commandment or prohibition, just knowing that it is from Allah and His Prophet (peace be upon him) should be enough for us.

Clothes to cover our bodies

In Islam there are certain parts of our bodies we must cover when we are in public. For women this is everything apart from their face, hands and feet. This includes a Hijab (headscarf) to cover their hair. For men it is between their navel and knees (although this doesn't allow them to walk about topless without good reason). The clothes that are used to cover these areas should not be so tight that the shape of the body beneath the clothes can be seen, and also should not be see-through so that skin can be seen seen through them. This is because the clothes we wear should hide our private parts and the other parts of our bodies which are only meant to be seen by our husbands or wives, or other close relatives. At home or with our family we can wear less clothes, or different types of clothes.

Children of Adam, We've inspired you with the idea of clothing for adornment and to cover your nakedness... (Qur'an 7:26)

...they shouldn't expose their beauty in public, except what is normally showing; and cover their bosoms with headscarves... (Qur'an 24:31)

Prophet, tell your wives, daughters, and the believer's wives to draw their overcoats close around... (Qur'an 33:59)

Syedatuna Asma bint Abu Bakr (may Allah be pleased with her) entered upon the Prophet (peace be upon him) while wearing transparent garments. He turned his face away and said, "O Asma! If a woman has reached puberty nothing should be seen of her body except this and this," and he pointed to his face and hands. (Abu Dawood)

Our bodies are a most precious gift

If we had a precious jewel we would not show it off to everyone. We would keep it safe and hidden, especially if we were taking it outside. We would only let some special people see it. Allah has made our bodies like this, they are very special things which we should be grateful for, which includes taking care of them and not showing them off to just anyone.

For the same reason, Allah tells men and women that when they are in public, they should keep their eyes down, and men should not stare at other women, and women should not stare at other men.

Tell believing men to lower their gaze and be modest; that is the best for them. Allah is aware of what they do. And tell believing women to lower their gaze and be modest... (Qur'an 24:30-31)

We should be mindful of our intention. For example, wearing deodorant or perfume so other people close to you aren't bothered by the smell of your sweat, and instead can smell a nice smell is an act of charity, but if a man is wearing perfume so that women will be attracted to him, or a woman is wearing perfume so that men will be attracted to her, this will displease Allah.

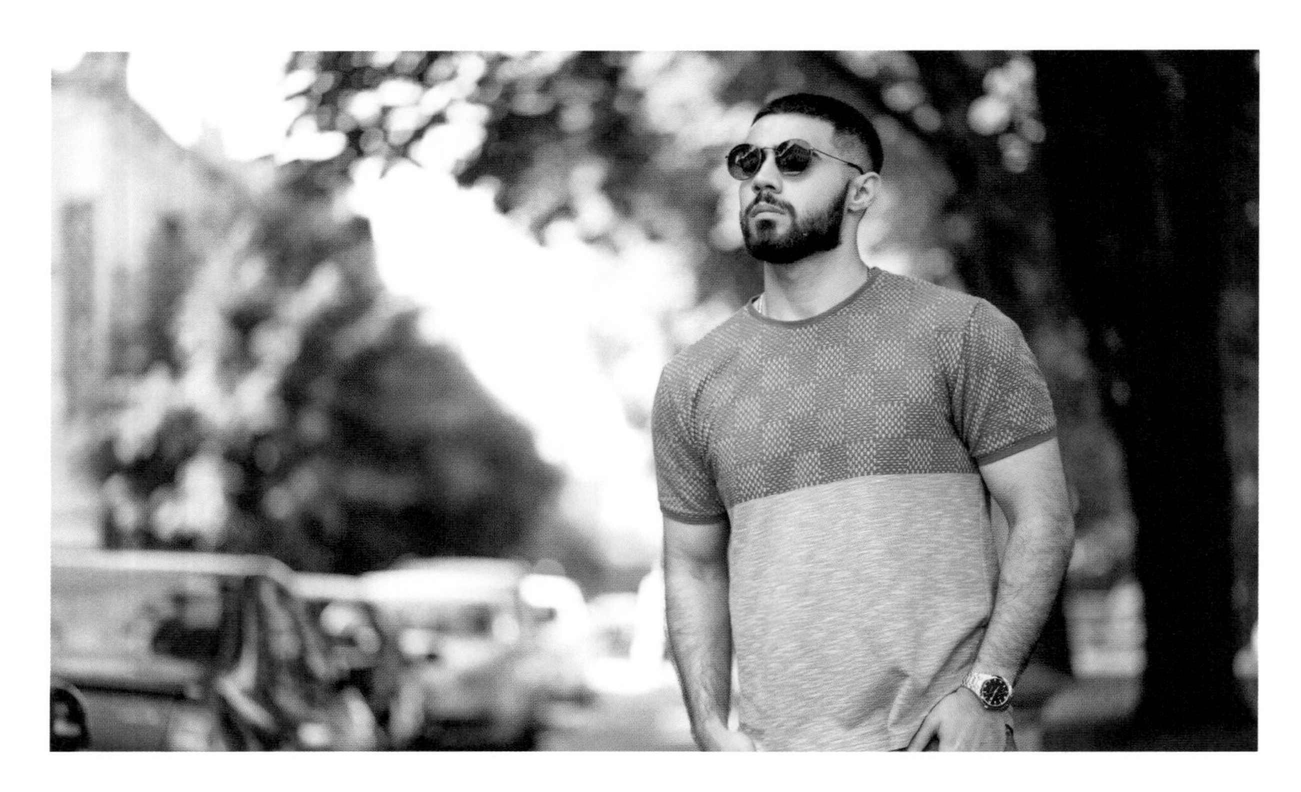

Syedina Abu Musa (may Allah be pleased with him) narrated that the Prophet (peace be upon him) said: "If a woman puts on perfume and passes by people so that they can smell her fragrance, then she is such and such," and he spoke sternly - meaning an adulteress. (Tirmidhi)

Women looking like men and men looking like women

Women should not wear clothes that make them look like men, and men should not wear clothes that make them look like women. Men are also not allowed to wear silk or gold jewellery. This is because Allah has made men and women different and special in their own ways. Allah does not like it when a man tries to make himself look like a woman, or a woman tries to make herself look like a man. Transvestites are an extreme example of this.

The Prophet (peace be upon him) cursed the man who wears women's clothing and the woman who wears men's clothing. (Abu Dawood)

The Prophet (peace be upon him) took some silk in his right hand and some gold in his left, declaring, "These two are Haram for the males among my followers." (Ahmad)

Avoiding extremes

Both men and women should wear clean clothes that are in good condition. In the same way you can show off by wearing very expensive

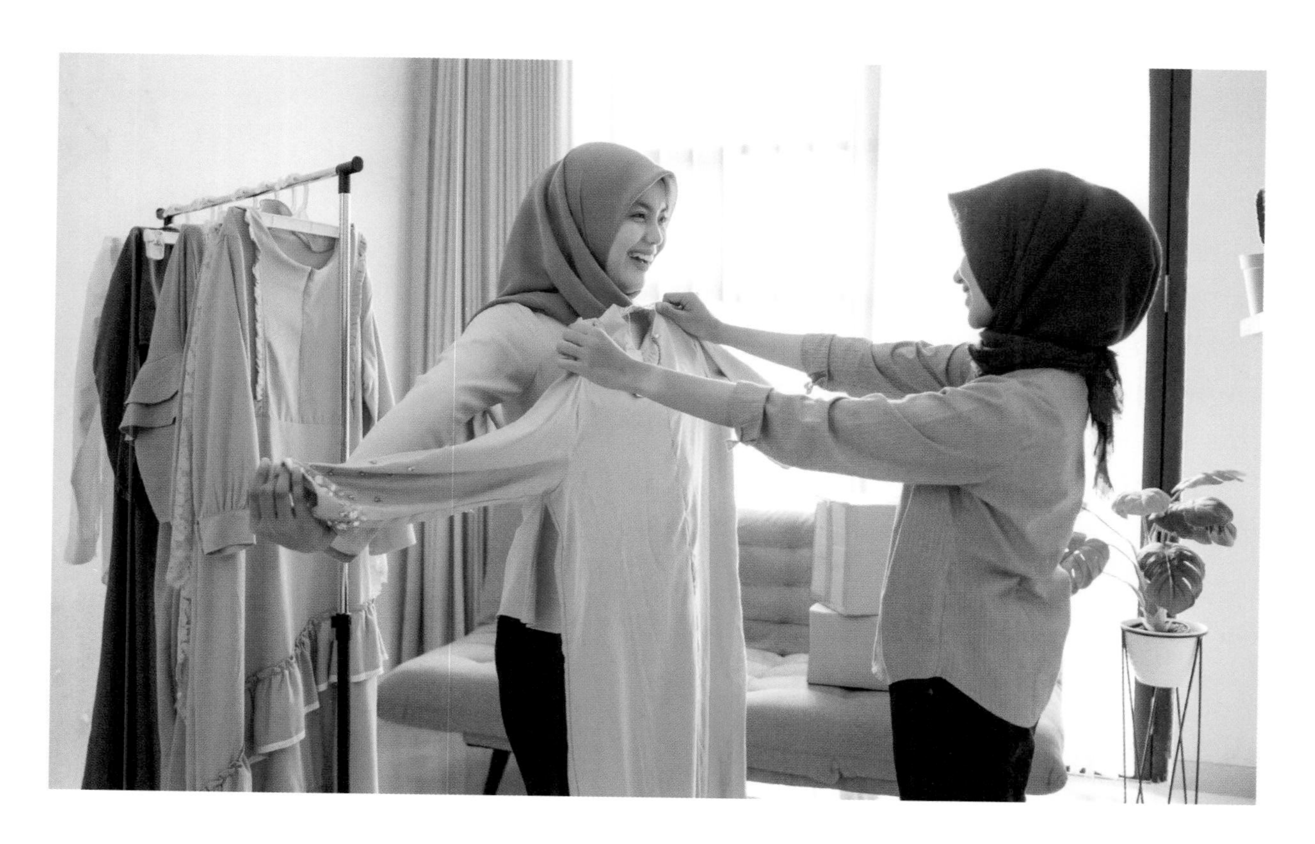

clothes, it is also possible to show off by wearing old, dirty clothes to make it seem like you are religious and not interested in worldly things. Showing off in any way is forbidden in Islam. The Prophet (peace be upon him) taught us to wear clothes according to what we can afford, so someone who is rich should wear nice clothes, but not to the point of extravagance.

The Prophet (peace be upon him) said: "Whoever wears a garment in vanity, Allah will make him wear a garment of humiliation on the Day of Resurrection, then He will set it ablaze with fire." (Ibn Majah)

The Prophet (peace be upon him) said: "No one who has an atom's-weight of arrogance in his heart will enter Paradise." A man said, "O Messenger of Allah, what if a man likes his clothes and his shoes to look good?" He said, "Allah is Beautiful and loves beauty. Arrogance means rejecting the truth and looking down on people." (Muslim)

Conclusion

If the rules above are followed, Islam allows us to wear whatever type of clothes we want, including different colours and styles from countries and cultures around the world; there is no one 'Islamic dress' code. While these rules may not apply to young children, it is wise for parents to explain why older family members dress the way they do, to follow the teachings of Allah and His Prophet (peace be upon him). For Muslims living in non-Muslim countries, we will be surrounded by people, including other Muslims who don't dress in this way. We might believe the way they are dressed is wrong, but this does not allow us to think less of them or persecute them, in the same way that we would not want others to treat us differently because of our 'Islamic' dress.

Questions

- What parts of her body does a Muslim woman need to cover?
- What parts of his body does a Muslim man need to cover?
- Is a Muslim woman allowed to wear clothes that make her look like a man?
- What types of clothes or jewellery are Muslim men not allowed to wear?
- What are the different ways people can show off with their clothes?

Activities

- Find pictures of Muslims from different countries to see the kind of clothes they wear, think about whether they are according to Islamic rules regarding dress
- When you next watch TV or go out, look at the clothes people wear, and think about why they would not be suitable for Muslim men or women
- When you next go to the Mosque or someone else's house, take a bath, brush your teeth, and wear some perfume so you smell nice

2.4

Relationships and Marriage

Objectives

- To understand why having a boyfriend or girlfriend is not allowed in Islam
- To explore the ways in which marriage protects us from the temptation of our Nafs and Shaitan
- To consider whether a person can be both Muslim and gay

Keywords

- Marriage
- Fornication
- Adultery
- Homosexuality

Adam and Eve, men and women

Allah created Syedina Adam (peace be upon him) as the first human and for a time he lived alone in Paradise. To ease his loneliness, Allah created Syedatuna Hawa (Eve – may Allah be pleased with her). She was his companion, and after they were married they had children together – in fact all of humanity are their descendants.

People, be mindful of your Lord, He created you from a single person and created his partner from him, and then from the pair He spread countless men and women throughout the world... (Qur'an 4:1)

Allah creates everything for a reason, it has a purpose. One of the purposes of creating men and women in the way He did, is that they form a pair. They are different but made to fit together, and when they do they can reproduce.

The Prophet (peace be upon him) stated: "Men and women are twin halves of each other." (Bukhari)

Boyfriends and girlfriends

Even from a young age, when boys and girls start spending time together, they can develop an attraction to each other. When this happens, they will want to spend more and more time together, looking at, and talking to each other. As this attraction grows they will want to hold hands, hug, and kiss. This will lead to exploring each other's bodies, and eventually sex (this is called fornication, or Zina).

All of these things feel very nice, which is why our Nafs (the part of our soul which produces 'animalistic' desires), will encourage us to do them. But as Muslims, such contact between men and women, or boys and girls, is only allowed within the confines of marriage. To do them

with anyone else is a major sin. This is why having a boyfriend or girlfriend is prohibited in Islam.

How our Nafs and Shaitan work against us

Along with our Nafs encouraging us to enjoy ourselves, the Shaitan wants us to sin, to displease Allah. This is why, when we are around members of the opposite sex it can be very difficult to control ourselves and not spend all our time staring at, and trying to talk to them. It is even harder if they are wearing revealing clothes and acting really friendly with us, making eye contact, laughing and joking with us, and perhaps even touching us, which might make us think they are purposefully flirting with us.

This is why we should not spend more time with members of the opposite sex than we have to (such as in school or at work). When we do spend time with them, we should try not to be alone with them, we should not stare at them, flirt with or touch them. These are things our Nafs and Shaitan will encourage us to do, because by doing them again and again, they will slowly lead us onto major sins.

How marriage can protect us

In the Qur'an and Hadith Muslims are encouraged to get married. Marriage provides a Halal avenue to indulge our Nafs and so saves us from committing major sins. This is why the Prophet described getting married as completing half of our religion.

Help the unmarried people amongst you to marry, and your righteous manservants and maidservants. Even if they are poor, Allah will make them self-sufficient through His grace... (Qur'an 24:32)

It is permissible for you to sleep with your wives during the nights of the fast – they are like a garment for you, as you are for them... (Qur'an 2:187)

Another of His signs is He created spouses for you from your own kind, in them you find comfort; and He nurtured love and kindness between you, in that are signs for the thinkers. (Qur'an 30:21)

The Prophet (peace be upon him) said: "O young men, whoever among you can afford it, let him get married, for it is more effective in lowering the gaze and guarding one's chastity. And whoever cannot afford it should fast, for it will be a shield for him." (Bukhari)

The Prophet (peace be upon him) said: "When Allah's servant marries, he has completed one half of the Religion. Thereafter let him fear Allah regarding the remaining half." (Al Bayhaqi)

Choosing someone to spend the rest of your life with is a major life decision. Therefore, as a Muslim if we like someone and think we might want to get married to them, it is important we spend time talking with them and getting to know what they are like. However, we should only do this with a chaperone. This makes it much easier to fight against our Nafs and Shaitan and not do something that would displease Allah.

The Prophet (peace be upon him) said: "No man is alone with a woman but the Shaitan is the third one present." (Ahmad)

Syedina al-Mugheerah ibn Shu'bah (may Allah be pleased with him) said: "I proposed marriage to a woman, and the Messenger of Allah (peace be upon him) said: 'Have you seen her?' I said, 'No.' He said, 'Look at her, because it is more fitting that love and compatibility be established between you.'" (Al Daraqutni)

Islam forbids forced marriages, where boys and girls are forced by their families, to marry people they might not know, or don't want to marry.

Syedatuna Aisha (may Allah be pleased with her) related that she once asked the Prophet: "In the case of a young girl whose parents marry her off, should her permission be sought or not?" He replied: "Yes, she must give her permission..." (Bukhari)

Shaitan never gives up

Even once we are married, it does not stop our Nafs and Shaitan from making us feel attracted to other people. This is more likely to happen if we spend a lot of time with other people, and not enough time with our spouse, or if there are lots of arguments and fights at home.

If we do not control our desires, and start having a relationship with someone other than our spouse, this is one of the most major sins in Islam (called adultery, also included in Zina), and at the time of the Prophet (peace be upon him) the punishment for this was for both of the people to receive the death penalty. The punishment was so severe to warn us regarding the magnitude of the sin and how much Allah hates it, and to act as a deterrent to stop others from doing the same thing (for more information see chapter on Hudud punishments).

You shall not go near adultery; it is indecency and an evil way of life. (Qur'an 17:32)

The Prophet (peace be upon him) said, "The one who commits illegal sexual intercourse is not a believer at the time of committing illegal sexual intercourse...Yet, (the gate of) repentance is open thereafter." (Bukhari)

Homosexuality

Sometimes, instead of boys and girls feeling attracted to each other (called heterosexuality), boys can feel attracted to other boys, and girls can feel attracted to other girls. This is called homosexuality, or being gay or lesbian. Some people feel attracted to both boys and girls (called bisexuality).

In Islam, we believe that having these kinds of feelings is a test from Allah. Homosexual marriages are not allowed in Islam. Therefore, even if you have homosexual feelings, you would not be able to act upon them without displeasing Allah. In the Qur'an we are told the story of the Prophet Lut (Lot - peace be upon him), whose people practiced homosexuality causing Allah to punish them. Having homosexual feelings is not a sin, and if you pray to Allah to help you and you do not act upon your feelings, Allah will be pleased with you.

And remember Lut, when he said to his people, "Why do you commit indecent acts that have no precedence anywhere in the whole world? You approach men with lust rather than women. You've gone to excess in satisfying your sexual appetites." (Qur'an 7:80-81)

We gave Lut authority and knowledge, and rescued him from a town which practised filthy acts of indecency; they were sinful people. (Qur'an 21:74)

The Prophet (peace be upon him) said: "There is nothing I fear for my ummah more than the deed of the people of Lut." (Tirmidhi)

The Prophet (peace be upon him) said: "A man should not look at the private parts of another man, and a woman should not look at the private parts of another woman." (Abu Dawood)

In the world we live in today homosexual relationships are very common and most non-Muslims believe there is nothing wrong with it. As Muslims, we believe homosexual relationships are wrong. But this does not mean we should think less of or persecute people who have homosexual feelings or are in a homosexual relationship. While we might believe that they are disobeying Allah, we should still love them as Allah's creation and behave with the best of manners, as did the Prophet (peace be upon him) with everyone around him, regardless of their race, religion, and actions. We should pray for Allah to guide them.

Conclusion

As Muslims our purpose in life is to please Allah by following His commandments and avoiding His prohibitions. If we strive to do this He will reward us with Paradise, but if we displease Allah He will punish us with Hell. This is true for every part of our lives, including our romantic relationships. If we ignore Allah, and instead follow our desires under the command of our Nafs and Shaitan, then we are trading an everlasting life of happiness in the hereafter for a finite amount of pleasure in this life.

Questions

- Why are we not allowed to have boyfriends or girlfriends in Islam?
- What is forced marriage, and does Islam allow this?
- What is the Islamic way of getting to know someone to see if we want to marry them?
- Which two enemies should we be careful about when we are around members of the opposite sex?
- Is homosexuality allowed in Islam?
- How should our behaviour be with people who are gay, lesbian, or bisexual?

Activities

- Talk to adults in your family about how they met their partners and got married
- If you see someone being bullied because they are homosexual, stand up for them
- Avoid using the word 'gay' (or any such word) as an insult

3. THE ISLAMIC PERSPECTIVE ON ADDICTIVE AND HARMFUL PRACTICES

3.1

Overeating and Obesity

Objectives

- To understand why overeating is disliked in Islam
- To explore the eating habits of the Prophet (peace be upon him)
- To consider the consequences on an individual and societal level of overeating

Keywords

- Overeating
- Overweight
- Obesity
- Health

How overeating leads to obesity and why that is bad for us

Overeating leads to gaining weight and obesity. This is because the food we eat contains calories (energy). If the amount of energy going into our body is more than the energy our body is using (e.g. in moving around, doing exercise), then we store that extra energy by converting it to fat. It does this in case we run out of food in the future, so our body can use its fat stores to stay alive. If on a regular basis our energy intake is higher than our energy use, our fat stores and therefore, weight will keep increasing and eventually we will become obese. The less exercise we do and the more fatty and sugary foods we eat, the faster this will happen.

Being obese increases our risks of many health problems including osteoarthritis, high blood pressure, heart disease, type 2 diabetes, stroke, heart attack, cancer, and psychological problems such as low self-esteem and depression. On average, people who are obese have 20 years less of healthy living than non-obese people and die 8 years sooner.

What Islam teaches us about overeating

In the Qur'an Allah tells us that He doesn't like people who eat and drink too much, and that out of all the things He has provided for us to eat, we should choose food that is good for us.

Believers, eat the wholesome foods We provide you and thank Allah... (Qur'an 2:172)

People, eat of what is lawful and wholesome on Earth... (Qur'an 2: 168)

...eat and drink, but don't squander; Allah dislikes the squanderers. (Qur'an 7:31)

The Prophet (peace be upon him) told us that the worst container a person can fill is his stomach, and that we should only eat as much as is needed to not collapse from hunger. But if we must fill it, then we should fill one third with food, one third with water, and one third with air.

The Prophet (peace be upon him) said, "The son of Adam cannot fill a vessel worse than his stomach, as it is enough for him to take a few bites to straighten his back. If he cannot do it, then he may fill a third with his food, a third with his drink, and a third with his breath." (Tirmidhi)

So Allah and His Prophet (peace be upon him) are telling us it is better to eat less than more, and the most we should eat and drink should still only fill 2/3rd of our stomach. The Prophet (peace be upon him) also encouraged staying fit and active, he told us that Allah loves all believers but the strong believer more than the weak believer.

The Prophet (peace be upon him) said: "A strong believer is better and is more lovable to Allah than a weak believer..." (Muslim)

Once the Prophet (peace be upon him) saw an overweight man and told him that if he did not have a paunch (belly fat) it would be better for him.

On seeing an overweight man, the Prophet (peace be upon him) said: "If you did not have a paunch it would be better for you." (Al Haythami)

The Prophet's wife, Syedatuna Aisha (may Allah be pleased with her) said that after the Prophet passed away (peace be upon him), the first test for the Muslims was being able to fill their stomachs with food, which causes the bodies to become fat, the heart to harden, and not being able to control their desires (the Nafs).

Syedatuna Aisha (may Allah be pleased with her) said: "The first calamity for this Ummah after the death of its Prophet (peace be upon him) will be satiety, for when people's stomachs are full, their bodies will grow fat, and their hearts will become weakened and their desires will grow wild." (Bukhari)

During the reign of the third caliph, Syedina Umar (May Allah be pleased with him), he came across a man with a big belly. The man said it was a blessing from Allah but Syedina Umar corrected him, that in truth it was a punishment.

The Prophet (peace be upon him) said, "Verily, the people who ate to their fill the most in this world will be the hungriest on the Day of Resurrection." (Ibn Majah)

How did the Prophet (peace be upon him) eat?

The Prophet (peace be upon him) also taught us how to eat. He would always recite the name of Allah before starting (Bismillah), eat while sitting (not leaning back or lying down), using three fingers of his right hand, and from the food that was in front of him and on his side of the plate. He would use a small dish to eat in and so his portion sizes were small. His diet very infrequently contained meat, which meant most of his meals were vegetarian, and the bread he ate was wholegrain. He would never criticise the food he was given, but would leave it if he disliked it. After he finished eating he would praise Allah and give thanks for the food. He would regularly fast. The only time he would eat until he was full was when he was a guest, as a way of honouring his host and showing that he liked their food. If we followed the advice of Allah and Sunnah of our Prophet (peace be upon him) we would not overeat and become overweight.

The Prophet (peace be upon him) said to his step-son Syedina Umar ibn Abi Salamah when he was eating with him: "Say Bismillah and eat from that which is in front of you in the dish." (Bukhari)

The Prophet (peace be upon him) said, "I do not eat reclining." (Bukhari)

Narrated Syedina Anas (may Allah be pleased with him): "To the best of my knowledge, the Prophet did not take his meals in a big tray at all, nor did he ever eat well-baked thin bread, nor did he ever eat at a dining table." (Bukhari)

Narrated Syedina Abu Hazim, that he asked Syedina Sahl (may Allah be pleased with them both), "Did you use white flour during the lifetime of the Prophet?" Syedina Sahl replied, "No." (Bukhari)

Narrated Syedina Abu Hurayrah (may Allah be pleased with him): The Prophet never criticized any food (he was invited to), but he used to eat if he liked the food, and leave it if he disliked it. (Bukhari)

The Prophet (peace be upon him), never ate to his fill of bread or meat unless he was eating with people. (Shama'il Muhammadiyah)

The Prophet (peace be upon him) said: "Allah is pleased with His slave when he eats something and praises Him for it, or drinks something and praises Him for it." (Muslim)

Why overeating is disliked by Allah and His Prophet (peace be upon him)

In Islam we are forbidden from harming our bodies and our health. These are precious gifts from Allah. Therefore, by eating too much to the extent of becoming obese we are being ungrateful to Allah and this is a sin.

If you are unthankful, then Allah has no need of you; He's not pleased with the lack of acknowledgement from His servants... (Qur'an 39:7)

Islam also teaches us to look after our neighbours, to make sure we are not filling our stomachs while they are going to bed hungry. It teaches us that the poor and needy have a right to our wealth, encouraging us to give charity. How are we doing this if we are overeating on a regular basis while there are poor people in our neighbourhoods struggling to buy food, having to use food banks, homeless people on every street corner, and millions of starving children all over the world?

...the worshippers, who perform their prayer constantly, in whose wealth is a due share for the beggar and the deprived... (Qur'an 70:24-25)

The Prophet (peace be upon him) said: "A man is not a believer who fills his stomach while his neighbour is hungry." (Al Albani)

If the money we spend on buying all this extra food could instead be donated to charity, imagine how much that would please Allah, while at the same time improve our health.

...Whatever good things you give in charity will benefit yourselves; that is, if you give seeking only Allah's pleasure. Whatever good things you give in charity will be rewarded, and you will not be short-changed in the least. (Qur'an 2:272)

Furthermore, there is also the extra cost to the healthcare system of treating obesity related diseases, money which could otherwise be spent on other things. Another effect of overeating is that with a full stomach you start to feel sleepy, or if you've eaten too much it can cause indigestion. This makes it more difficult to concentrate in your worship, especially if praying during the night.

Conclusion

We should be careful of not developing a habit of overeating. This will lead to us becoming overweight with all its associated health problems. If this is something we are careless about we are being ungrateful to Allah for the immense blessing of our bodies and our health and going against the teachings of our Prophet (peace be upon him). If instead we develop a habit of keeping at least a 1/3rd of our stomach empty whenever we eat and drink and doing regular exercise, we will remain fit and healthy. We will also find worshipping Allah easier and more fulfilling, and the money we save can be used to help the poor and needy.

For some people this is easier than others, but even in making this effort is a blessing for us, it is a Jihad (struggle) against our Nafs (desires) and a way to draw closer to Allah. This is why we should never look down upon or persecute people who are struggling with being overweight. This is not following the example of the Prophet (peace be upon), instead we should encourage them and support them in their efforts to lose weight.

Questions

- Why do people become overweight?
- What does Islam teach us about overeating?
- What can we do to stop ourselves from overeating?
- How does overeating affect our worship?

Activities

- Do some research on how the different types of food we eat are used by our bodies
- Watch a documentary about obese people and how their weight affects their life
- If someone is being bullied due to their weight, stand up for them

3.2

Alcohol, Recreational Drugs and Smoking

Objectives

- To understand why drinking alcohol, taking recreational drugs and smoking are not allowed in Islam
- To explore the effects of engaging in these activities on a person, their family, and the wider society
- To consider the financial cost of these activities, and what better way that money might be spent

Keywords

- Alcohol
- Drugs
- Smoking

Alcohol

Drinking even a small amount of any type of alcoholic drink is Haram (impermissible):

Believers, wine, gambling by drawing lots, the use of pagan sacrificial altars, or foretelling the future with arrows are filthy works of Satan; reject them so that you may succeed in life. (Qur'an 5:90)

The Prophet (peace be upon him) said: "Every liquor which intoxicates is forbidden." (Bukhari)

The Prophet (peace be upon him) said: "Abstain from alcohol because it is the key (source) of all evils." (Abu Dawood)

The Prophet (peace be upon him) said: "...When one drinks alcohol, he is not a believer..." (Bukhari)

One of the Divine wisdoms behind this blanket prohibition is that the amount of alcohol needed to become drunk differs for everyone. Furthermore, becoming drunk is a gradual process of intoxication, however much you drink will have some effect on your senses (hence why drink driving is illegal due to the increased risk of road accidents). Alcohol is also an addictive substance, so even though you may plan to drink a small amount, as you start to become intoxicated it is likely you will drink more. All of this means this means that many people who drink alcohol end up becoming drunk even though this was not their intention when they started drinking. Once they are intoxicated, they lose their inhibitions and are more likely to engage in prohibited acts such as arguing, fighting, promiscuity, and not fulfilling religious obligations, such as praying Salah.

The addictive nature of alcohol means a small but significant proportion of drinkers become alcoholics (with some studies quoting figures of nearly 25% of adults under 30 meeting their definition of alcoholism). Alcoholism can destroy individual lives and families through the amount of time and money wasted on drinking. Those who are not able to stop, end up dying prematurely due to liver failure and other associated health

problems. Therefore, the Islamic prohibition also relates to the principle of not harming our bodies, which are gifts from Allah and ours to take care of, not abuse.

...do not cast yourselves into the jaws of destruction by your own hands... (Qur'an 2:195)

Recreational drugs

Taking recreational (non-medicinal) drugs is Haram. This is because all types of recreational drugs, whatever their route of entry into the body (e.g. ingested, inhaled, injected) cause intoxication, which has been clearly prohibited by the Prophet (peace be upon him):

The Prophet (peace be upon him) said: "...every intoxicant is unlawful." (Muslim)

Recreational drugs are also addictive, and in the section above on alcohol we have already discussed the harmful effects of addictive and intoxicating substances. A further harmful effect of some recreational drugs is that they can cause paranoid thoughts or hallucinations, and cause, as well as exacerbate mental illness, such as psychosis. A small but significant proportion of recreational drug users die due to overdosing (in 2017 there were 8,200 such deaths reported in the European Union, with the majority of people in their thirties and forties).

Cigarettes

Cigarettes/cigars are not intoxicants like alcohol or recreational drugs; however, they are very harmful to our health. Even smoking pure tobacco (as is the case with some types of cigarettes, and with Hookah/Shisha) causes inhalation of harmful substances such as tar (used to make road surfaces) and carbon monoxide (which stops your blood cells from being able to carry oxygen), let alone all the other substances found in most cigarettes including nicotine (highly addictive when inhaled), arsenic (used in rat poison), and ammonia (used in toilet cleaner). Smoking eventually leads to death, through development of health conditions such as chronic obstructive pulmonary disease, heart attack, stroke, and lung cancer.

Furthermore, people who breathe in your second hand smoke (most often close family and friends) are also exposed to the hundreds of toxic chemicals contained within cigarette smoke. Research has shown that this increases the risk of sudden infant death syndrome (SIDS) in babies, can exacerbate asthma and common respiratory infections in children (meaning they get more sick, require more medicine, and take longer to get better), and cause heart disease, stroke and lung cancer in adults who may never have smoked themselves.

More recently, electronic cigarettes (vaping) are readily available and touted as a healthier alternative. While this assertion is true (since they don't contain tobacco or produce carbon monoxide, and much lower levels of toxic chemicals are found within their smoke compared to cigarette smoke), compared to not smoking at all they still cause harm to your body. And since they are a relatively new product, there is no data on the effects of long-term use. Currently, the NHS recommends their use to help people stop smoking cigarettes (since they contain nicotine and also mimic the act of smoking).

Due to the obvious harm smoking causes to our bodies, and to those around us, there are Fatwas (legal pronouncements by Muftis; experts in religious law) from several countries (e.g. Saudi Arabia, Jordan, Egypt, Malaysia, Indonesia, the Philippines, etc.) that it is a Haram activity.

Conclusion

In Islam all intoxicants are Haram, regardless of the amount being consumed which may not have an intoxicating effect by itself. We are also not allowed to harm our bodies for recreational purposes, this is a sign of extreme ingratitude to Allah for the immense blessing of good health that He has bestowed upon us. Furthermore, substances such as alcohol, recreational drugs and cigarettes are addictive and costly, by indulging in them not only are we displeasing Allah, but we are also wasting our time and money, which could otherwise be spent with our families, and in His worship.

The Prophet (peace be upon him) said: "A person will not be dismissed (on the Day of Judgement) until he has been asked about four things: his life and in what he spent it, his knowledge and what he did with it, his wealth, from where he acquired it and on what he spent it, and his body and how he wore it out." (Tirmidhi)

Questions

- How do people behave when they are drunk?
- Is drinking too much alcohol bad for your health?
- What are some of the harmful effects of taking recreational drugs?
- What harmful substances do cigarettes contain?
- What health problems do smokers have?
- Why is alcohol, drugs and smoking Haram?

Activities

- Watch a video of how people behave when they are drunk
- Watch a documentary of how alcoholism affects people's lives
- Watch a video of how people behave when they are under the influence of drugs
- Watch a documentary of how drug addiction affects people's lives
- Watch a video of what cigarette smoke does to a smoker's lungs
- Watch a documentary of how chronic smoking affects people's lives

3.3

Gambling

Objectives

- To understand why gambling is prohibited in Islam
- To explore the effects of gambling on a person and their family and friends
- To consider the difference between gambling and using that money to help others

Keywords

- Gambling
- Casino
- Betting
- Lottery

What is gambling?

Gambling (Maisir) is when a game of chance is played for money or some other type of wealth (such as a possession). Whether you win or lose, the game of chance will determine whether you win money (from the people you are playing against, or the establishment such as a casino or betting shop) or lose the money you wagered. Examples of this can include playing a poker game against your friends, betting on a horse, or buying a lottery ticket.

Problems caused by gambling

So gambling is where you are risking the wealth that Allah has blessed you with to try and win more wealth, based on luck and in some games, your level of skill. Most people, before they begin gambling, decide how much money they are willing to lose before they would stop. But most gamblers, when they've reached that threshold, decide to continue gambling because they believe that with the next turn their luck will change and they will win back the money they've lost.

In this way gambling is addictive, there is always the chance to win a lot of money by spending a little, by taking another turn. However, for most people, this just means they keep losing more and more money. This addictive nature means it is difficult for gamblers to stop gambling even when it is causing significant problems in their lives. Most gamblers end up penniless and even in debt, having gambled away money they do not have (using credit card, or loans). This would have been money they could have spent on themselves or their families. They can be left unable to buy food and often homeless due to being unable to afford their rent or mortgage payments. This not only affects them but also their families. Many marriages in which the husband or wife gambles end up in divorce.

Why is gambling Haram?

Allah tells us in the Qur'an that Shaitan uses gambling to stop us from performing Salah and remembering Allah. People who gamble with each other might be friends to start with, but because they are winning money off each other this can lead to feelings of betrayal and hatred, and lead to enmity and even violence. Allah warns us about this in the Qur'an, that gambling is a tool Shaitan uses for this purpose. Allah describes it as an abomination (something that is disgusting, hateful), and a handiwork of Shaitan.

Believers, wine, gambling by drawing lots, the use of pagan sacrificial altars, or foretelling the future with arrows are filthy works of Satan; reject them so that you may succeed in life. Satan wishes to sow enmity and hatred between you using wine and gambling, and to divert you from the remembrance of Allah and performance of the prayer. So, will you not stop? (Qur'an 5:90-91)

Some people are very good at gambling and use it to become wealthy. But any wealth we gain from gambling is Haram and will not have any Barakat in it (it will not be of any benefit for us). We might use that money to buy food for ourselves and our families, but the Prophet (peace be upon him) told us that any flesh fed with Haram will end up in the Hellfire, and it is a cause for our Duas to not be accepted. Even if we don't use that money on ourselves or our family and decide to give it to charity, it will not be accepted.

The Prophet (peace be upon him) said: "No flesh grows that was nourished by that which is unlawful, but the Fire is more appropriate for it." (Tirmidhi) The Prophet (peace be upon him) mentioned [the case] of a man

who, having journeyed far, is dishevelled and dusty, and who spreads out his hands to the sky saying "O Lord! O Lord!" while his food is Haram, his drink is Haram, his clothing is Haram, and he has been nourished with Haram, so how can [his supplication] be answered? (Muslim)

The Prophet (peace be upon him) said, "A slave (of Allah) who acquires Haram wealth and gives charity from it, it is not accepted from him. If he spends from it, he does not have any blessing (Barakah) in it. If he leaves it behind him (i.e. he dies) it will be a means of taking him to the fire (of Hell). Verily, Allah does not wipe out evil deed with evil deed; instead, He wipes out evil deed with good deed. Indeed, the repulsive does not wipe out the repulsive." (Ahmad)

Conclusion

Gambling is a sin that will cause most people to become poor and lonely, to the extent of losing everything they have and even becoming homeless. However, this pales in comparison to the spiritual damage they are doing themselves that will lead to punishment in the afterlife. Therefore, even for those who are good at it, who believe they are winning, are in fact of the losers in both this life and the next.

Questions

- What is gambling?
- Are we gambling when we buy a lottery ticket?
- Are most gamblers wealthy people?
- Why does the Shaitan want us to gamble?
- If we are good at gambling and win lots of money, as Muslims, what can we use that money for?

Activities

- Do some research on the probability of winning the lottery
- Watch a documentary about how gambling affects people's lives
- Watch a documentary about casinos, and how they are designed to make people gamble and lose money
- Any money that you were thinking of using to gamble, give it in charity instead

3 . 4

Tattoos and Body Piercings

Objectives

- To understand why permanent tattoos are prohibited in Islam
- To explore why some body piercings are allowed but others are not
- To consider why someone might regret getting a permanent tattoo or body piercing

Keywords

- Tattoos
- Temporary
- Permanent
- Piercings

What are tattoos?

Tattoos are a type of body modification which involves drawing on the skin. They can be temporary (such as Henna/Mehndi), or permanent. Permanent tattoos are created by inserting ink or dye underneath the top layer of skin. This is done using needles (by hand or with a machine).

Changing our bodies

The Prophet (peace be upon him) cursed the one who gets a tattoo and the one who tattoos other people. In another Hadith it is said this is because these people are changing the creation of Allah.

Syedina Abu Juhayfah (may Allah be pleased with him) said: "The Prophet (peace be upon him) cursed those ladies who practice tattooing and those who get themselves tattooed." (Bukhari)

In the Qur'an Allah tells us that we should not desire to change or alter His creation, and in fact this is one of the ways Shaitan makes us displease Allah.

Allah has cursed him (Satan) for saying: "I will take an allotted share of Your servants; and I will lead them astray and give them false hopes and I will order them to slit the ears of cattle and to tinker with Allah's creation." (Qur'an 4:118-119)

This does not apply to temporary tattoos that fade from the skin within a few days. Given the above, getting a permanent tattoo is a sinful act and forbidden in Islam.

Damaging our bodies

Getting a tattoo can be a very painful procedure, depending on which part of the body is involved, how many nerve endings are in the skin and how much fat is under the skin. Pain is our body's way of telling us it is hurt, to make us move away from what is causing us pain, to stop our body from getting damaged (this is why we quickly pull our hand away from a hot object). So getting a tattoo involves hurting our bodies, even if the damage is not serious. Islam prohibits us from harming our bodies, especially just for cosmetic reasons.

Furthermore, the skin bleeds when it is pierced during the procedure so there is a risk of transmission of blood borne diseases (such as HIV or Hepatitis) if the needle used is not sterile. If the skin is not cleaned adequately and taken care of for days or even weeks after the procedure, it can get infected and need treatment with antibiotics.

The Prophet (peace be upon him) said, "There are two gifts which many men are unmindful about – good health and leisure." (Bukhari)

The Prophet (peace be upon him) said, "No supplication is more pleasing to Allah than a request for good health." (Tirmidhi)

That Day, you will be questioned about all the blessings you enjoyed. (Qur'an 102:8)

Showing off and exposing our bodies

Many people get tattoos to show off to others. They might get them on parts of their bodies which Muslims are meant to keep covered in front of everyone other than their spouses (between navel and knees for a man, and everything apart from face and hands for a woman). This is different from women getting Henna tattoos on their hands at times of celebration, such as Eid or weddings, which is allowed.

Wasting money

Tattoos are expensive, especially if they are large and/or detailed. On average they will cost between £50 to £100 but can cost up to and above £1000. Imagine if instead of spending this money on a tattoo you gave it in charity, helping the poor and needy? Consider how much that would please Allah. Even if not, you could spend that money on something else nice for yourself that is not Haram.

...don't spend your wealth wastefully. Those who waste are the brothers of Satan, and Satan is the most unthankful to His Lord. (Qur'an 17:26-27)

...Whatever good things you give in charity will benefit yourselves; that is, if you give seeking only Allah's pleasure. Whatever good things you give in charity will be rewarded, and you will not be short-changed in the least. (Qur'an 2:272)

Removing tattoos

Many people who get a tattoo regret it later in life. However, to remove it requires laser treatment. Depending on the size and colours used, it can take up to 10 sessions to remove one tattoo, with about a month's gap in between each one. Each session costs around £50, so it can be very expensive and very painful. The underlying lasered skin will be very red and sore, it can develop a rash and blisters and there is a risk of infection if not kept clean. There is no guarantee the treatment will fully work, some colours may be left in the skin and there is also a small chance you are left with permanent scarring.

Body piercings

Body piercings are another type of body modification, generally done for the purpose of wearing jewellery (such as pierced ears, nose, lips, tongue, navel, etc.). Therefore, the same principles that apply to permanent tattoos apply to body piercings, and it is not allowed because we are changing Allah's creation (our bodies) for solely cosmetic reasons.

Many parts of the body that are pierced are very sensitive, and the procedure involves a great deal of pain and risk of infection. Putting our health at risk without good reason is forbidden in Islam. The body part being pierced may also be one that is meant to be kept covered. Even if an intention is made that the piercing is only for the purpose of showing your spouse, you would still have had to expose yourself to the person who did the piercing, which is Haram.

Are any piercings allowed?

The only exception to this is ear piercing for women. During the life of the Prophet (peace be upon him) women practised ear piercing and he did not forbid this. This means it is permissible.

Some schools of religious law say that this exception is not just for ears, but any part of the body that is pierced for the purposes of wearing jewellery in your culture. However, there are some rules regarding this, some of which we've already discussed. Furthermore, the piercing should not involve an area of the body that generally, non-Muslims get pierced and Muslims don't get pierced. This is because the Prophet (peace be upon him) forbade us from copying the actions of non-Muslims or trying to imitate them to make ourselves like them.

The Prophet (peace be upon him) said: "Whoever imitates a people is one of them." (Abu Dawood)

It should also not be an area of the body which has a high risk of causing

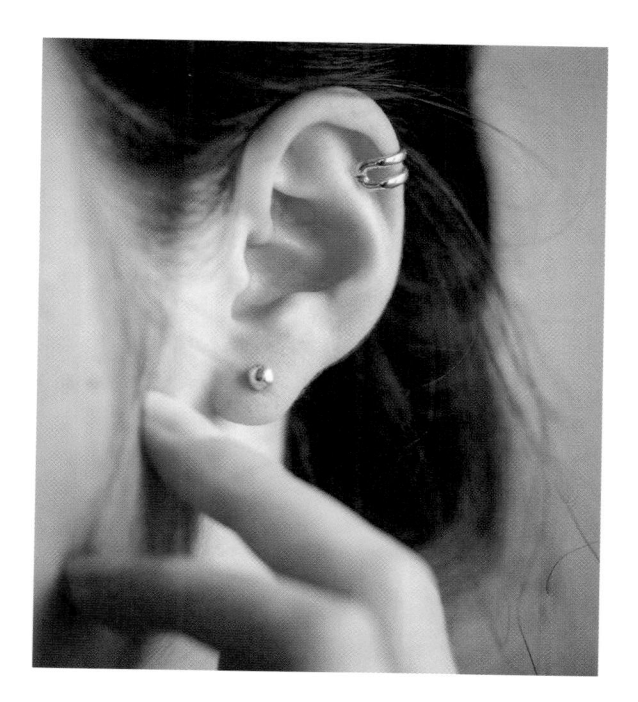

causing health problems by getting pierced. An example of a piercing practice which fulfils these criteria, is the side of their nose. An example of a piercing which would not fulfil these criteria and so would be forbidden for Muslim women to get would be nipple piercing.

Are men allowed body piercings?

Men are not allowed to pierce any part of their body. The purpose of piercing is to wear jewellery. The Prophet (peace be upon him) told us that Allah curses men who copy women. So if a man was to get one or both of his ears pierced to wear an earring (let alone any other area of his body), he would earn the curse of Allah.

The Prophet (peace be upon him) said: "Allah curses men who imitate women and women who imitate men." (Bukhari)

Conclusion

Allah has given us our bodies as a beautiful gift but He is our Lord and Creator, He is the one who owns us, we are His slaves. Therefore, this precious thing we have been entrusted with, which at the end of our lives will return back to Him, should be treated with the utmost respect to show our gratitude. If we try to change it by getting permanent tattoos and body piercings, we are disobeying Allah and not following the example set by the Prophet (peace be upon him). By doing this we will displease Allah, and what is to stop Him from taking our bodies away from us during this life, or punishing us in the afterlife?

Remember when your Lord declared, "If you are grateful, I will surely increase My favours to you, but if you are ungrateful, then My punishment is severe." (Qur'an 14:7)

Will it have been worth it for that tattoo or body piercing which you will most likely regret when you are older anyway?

Questions

- Why are permanent tattoos not allowed in Islam?
- If someone wants to get a tattoo removed, what does this involve?
- Why are body piercings not allowed in Islam?
- Are there any exceptions to this?
- Why are men not allowed to pierce their ears?

Activities

- Watch a documentary about tattoos
- Watch a documentary about body piercings

3.5

Pornography and Masturbation

Objectives

- To understand why pornography is prohibited in Islam
- To explore why masturbation is a harmful and addictive habit
- To consider how a person addicted to viewing pornography and masturbating can break these habits

Keywords

- Pornography
- Masturbation
- Zina
- Ghusl

What is pornography and why is it Haram?

Pornography refers to any material used for the purpose of sexually exciting the audience. Often, this involves showing the naked bodies of men and women and people engaged in sexual activity. Pornography can take the form of writing, pictures, photos, sound or speech, videos, or games.

Human beings are the most special creation of Allah. He granted us free will and by following His guidance and the example of the Prophet (peace be upon him) we can live a life of honour and dignity and rise higher in rank than the Angels. However, if we follow our Nafs and the whisperings of Shaitan we can sink to lower in rank than the animals.

We created man in the most beautiful form. (Qur'an 95:4)

We honoured the children of Adam...and favoured them above all Our creation. (Qur'an 17:70)

Haven't you considered how Allah made everything in the Heavens and the Earth serve your needs, and bestowed His gifts on you, visible and hidden?... (Qur'an 31:20)

And so it is that many of the Jinn and humans We've created are intended for Hell. They have brains which don't think, eyes that won't see, and ears that don't hear, such people are like cattle, even more dumb, worse than them; they are unaware of reality. (Qur'an 7:179)

Allah tells us in the Qur'an to lower our gazes and guard our private parts. Furthermore, we are told to cover our bodies using clothes. Islam teaches modesty and shamefulness, respect, honour and dignity for ourselves and our fellow human beings; pornography is the opposite of all this.

Tell believing men to lower their gaze and be modest; that is the best for them. Allah is aware of what they do. And tell believing women to lower their gaze and be modest; they shouldn't expose their beauty in public, except what is normally showing; and cover their bosoms with headscarves... (Qur'an 24:30-31)

Children of Adam, We've inspired you with the idea of clothing for adornment and to cover your nakedness... (Qur'an 7:26)

A lot of pornography includes men and women committing Zina (fornication and adultery). The Prophet told us that by viewing such things we are participating, by committing Zina with our eyes and minds. Therefore, in Islam any type of pornography is Haram. This means it is Haram for a Muslim to be involved in producing, distributing,

distributing, acting in, and looking at pornography.

You shall not go near adultery; it is indecency and an evil way of life. (Qur'an 17:32)

The Prophet (peace be upon him) said: "The adultery of the eye is the lustful look and the adultery of the ears is listening and the adultery of the tongue is immodest speech and the adultery of the hand is the lustful grip and the adultery of the feet is to walk (to the place where he intends to commit adultery) and the heart yearns and desires, and the private parts put this into effect or reject it." (Muslim)

What is masturbation and why is it Haram?

Masturbation is the practice of stimulating your genitals for sexual pleasure which may or may not lead to orgasm. Masturbation is practiced by both sexes and can be done via the finger or hands, or the use of objects.

According to the majority of Islamic scholars, masturbation is Haram. This ruling is taken from a passage in the Qur'an in which Allah tells the believers to guard their sexual organs from anyone or anything other than the people they can lawfully have a sexual relationship with (e.g. their spouse).

The believers will succeed: those who are humbly focused in their prayers; who turn away from meaningless activities; who give Zakat; who guard their modesty and sexual purity, except from their spouses or their maids, in which case they are free from blame – but whoever desires sexual gratification more than this will be a transgressor... (Qur'an 23:1-7)

This verse sets boundaries for what is allowed, and anything not specified is automatically prohibited. Therefore, masturbation is prohibited. However, some scholars believe that according to the principle of the lesser of two evils; if a person genuinely fears that without resorting to masturbation they will be unable to control their sexual desires and may commit Zina (sex outside of marriage), then it is permissible although severely

disliked. However, this would only apply if the person had already tried or was unable to follow the advice of the Prophet (peace be upon him) to get married or to fast (as a way of reducing sexual desire).

The Prophet (peace be upon him) said: "Whoever among you can afford to get married, let him do so, and whoever cannot afford it should fast, for it will be a restraint for him." (An Nasai)

The prohibition on masturbation is supported by another Qur'anic verse in which Allah tells us to remain chaste until we are able to get married.

And let those who lack the means to marry keep themselves chaste until Allah makes them self-sufficient through His grace. Allah is Vast, All-Knowing (Qur'an 24:33)

Some scholars have argued that being chaste means protecting your private parts from all prohibited, shameful acts (including masturbation), not just sexual intercourse outside of marriage. If we believe masturbation to be a shameful act, then many Qur'anic verses would apply to it, prohibiting us from partaking in such deeds.

...Stay well clear of gross indecency, whether openly or in secret... (Qur'an 6:151)

... He shall punish the evil, and richly reward the righteous: who avoid major sins and shameful deeds... (Qur'an 53:31-32)

Another reason why masturbation is prohibited is because it is normally practiced alongside the viewing of pornography.

Pornography and masturbation in today's world

In the current day and age, it is very easy to be exposed to pornography in our everyday lives, while we are doing normal everyday things. We can be walking or driving down the road and see a billboard on which a man or woman is wearing revealing clothing. While watching TV advertisements often contain scenes of men and women in their underwear. Many TV programs or movies we watch openly discuss masturbation and contain sex scenes. While browsing the internet, even if searching for pictures of something innocent, some of the results are likely to be pornographic.

Our Nafs will want us to look at these things and the Shaitan will encourage us. They will try to convince us that it doesn't matter if we have a quick look, that it is only natural to want to look at these things at our age and everybody does it, and that we can always ask Allah to forgive us later. They may encourage us to purposefully search for pornography and to masturbate.

This is very easy to do nowadays, our internet connection is on all the time and we all have phones, tablets or laptops on which we can easily find an endless supply of the most shameless kind of pornography. No-one will know what we are doing because we can do it in the privacy of our bedroom or bathroom, or anywhere else we are alone.

Even if people were to find out we looked at pornography and masturbated, no-one would say anything because in the world we live in today it is considered normal, even healthy for both men and women. They would say that if the people who are making pornography and the people who are viewing it and masturbating are enjoying themselves and doing it because they want to, then that is all that matters and we shouldn't feel guilty or ashamed of what we are doing.

Is watching pornography harmful?

Psychologists tell us that looking at pornography is addictive. The longer we spend viewing pornography, the more desensitised we become to the kind of things we are seeing, which means it won't stimulate us anymore. So over time we will need to keep finding different and more extreme pornography to keep stimulating us.

Children who view too much pornography can have trouble in their relationships later in life. Pornography is fake, it is made by actors, but children who view it start believing that this is the normal way men and women behave with each other, especially when having sex. This includes degrading and violent behaviour. There are many people who regret having looked at pornography when they were younger, because it has made it more difficult for them to have real life relationships. And even though they know it is harmful, they are addicted to it and find it very hard to stop.

Is masturbating harmful?

Masturbation is also addictive, especially if done in conjunction with viewing pornography. Once we have developed a strong habit it will be difficult to give up even if we want to. Excessive masturbation can impact on our daily lives, making us spend time alone indulging in this habit whereas we might have better spent that time studying, working, with family or friends, or worshipping Allah.

If we ejaculate as a result of masturbation it becomes necessary to perform Ghusl (full body ritual purification – a bath or shower) before we can pray, but even if we don't ejaculate, the release of pre-

ejaculatory fluid nullifies our Wudu (ritual ablution). If we do not perform Wudu or Ghusl before reciting the Qur'an or praying Salah our worship will not be accepted.

Excessive masturbation can have further negative consequences once we are married. Having developed such as strong habit it is likely we will continue it despite having a spouse with whom we can engage in permissible sexual activities. Furthermore, having become used to enjoying how we stimulate ourselves, there can be dissatisfaction and problems enjoying sex with our partners. Such things can lead to the breakdown of a marriage.

Are we ever really alone?

In Islam we don't believe we are alone even when there is no-one else around us. There are two Angels seated on our shoulders recording every good and bad deed that we do, which will be presented to us on the Day of Judgement.

Guardians standing over you are the noble scribes, who know what you do. (Qur'an 82:10-12)

...on Judgement Day, We shall bring out the document and spread it wide open before them; read you own document! You should be able to calculate your own account today. (Qur'an 17:13-14)

Today We shall seal their mouths; their hands will speak, and their feet will bear witness to what they did. (Qur'an 36:65)

So every time we disobeyed Allah by looking at pornography and masturbating will be written in our book of deeds, and on the Day of Judgement our eyes and hands will tell of every shameless thing we looked at and did.

Disobeying our Creator

Allah is also watching us and knows not only everything that we do, but also every thought and feeling we

have. As Muslims we believe that Allah is our Creator, the One who gave us life and everything that we have. The purpose of our life is to worship Him, to please Him, to earn His Paradise. If we truly believe this then how can we disobey and displease Him by looking at pornography and masturbating, knowing they are sinful acts?

Being grateful for our blessings

Do we not consider how immense a blessing it is that Allah has given us eyes? Have you ever imagined what the life of a blind person is like? When we use these eyes to look at pornography we are being ungrateful to Allah, by using His gift in a way that displeases Him. What is to stop our Lord and Creator from taking away His blessing from us? Allah tells us that if we are grateful, He will increase His blessings upon us. If we save our eyes from looking at such shameless things, Allah might bless us to be able to see special things, like the Prophet (peace be upon him) in our dreams.

Remember when your Lord declared, "If you are grateful, I will surely increase My favours to you, but if you are ungrateful, then My punishment is severe." (Qur'an 14:7)

The Prophet (peace be upon him) said: "Whoever sees me in a dream has actually seen me. Satan cannot take my form." (Bukhari)

Similarly, consider what immense blessings are contained within our hands and our genitalia. There are people who are born without hands, or lose them through accidents or diseases – consider how difficult their life is compared to your own. Should we not be grateful to the One who has given us our hands by using them in ways that would please Him?

Our genitalia allow us to partake in sex – a most amazing, unique, sensory experience, which can result in one of the most special and meaningful experiences of our lives – to have children. Again, there are many people who are bereft of these blessings of Allah due to physical and psychological problems. How would we feel if we were to lose these blessings through the actions of our own hands?

Is it worth it?

What do we gain from looking at pornography and masturbating? It might feel good while we are doing it, although if we are a good Muslim we will feel guilty afterwards about disobeying and displeasing Allah, and so overall we will actually feel worse than if we hadn't done it in the first place.

And what is the price we pay for this temporary, fleeting pleasure? As we commit sins our heart becomes covered with darkness and we fall further and further away from Allah. As we persevere in our sins, we stop feeling ashamed, we stop asking Allah for forgiveness. We lack concentration in the good deeds we deeds we do, and as our addiction grows stronger, we stop doing them altogether as we spend more and more of our time indulging in our sin. Even when we aren't actively engaged in it, our mind is preoccupied with it, until we have become a slave to it and even if we wanted to stop we couldn't. If we die in this state we will be punished in the grave, and on the Day of Judgement Allah will throw us into Hell. Is this worth it?

The Prophet (peace be upon him) said: "Verily, when the slave (of Allah) commits a sin, a black spot appears on his heart. When he refrains from it, seeks forgiveness and repents, his heart is polished clean. But if he returns, it increases until it covers his entire heart. And that is the 'Ran' which Allah mentioned: 'Nay, but on their hearts is the Ran which they used to earn (Qur'an 83:14).'" (Tirmidhi)

Conclusion

Islam is a religion of beauty which places a great deal of importance on modesty and shamefulness. Pornography and masturbation are the opposite of this and Haram for Muslims. The men and women who are involved in producing pornography, they are someone's son and daughter, someone's brother and sister, someone's mother and father. If that was your relative would you want others to masturbate while looking at them naked, engaged in sexual activities? If not, then should we be engaged in such acts?

Syedina Abu Umama Al-Bahily (may Allah be pleased with him) narrated that a young man came to the Prophet (peace be upon him) and said: "O Messenger of Allah, give me a permission to commit Zina." The Companions (may Allah be pleased with them all) turned to him and started rebuking him. The Prophet said: "Come closer." When the young man drew nearer to the Prophet and sat down, the Prophet asked him: "Would you like it for your mother?" The man answered: "No, by Allah. May Allah make me a protection for you!" The Prophet commented, "People also do not like it for their mothers." The Prophet added, "Would you like it for your daughter?" Again, the young man answered negatively. So, the Prophet said, "People too would not love it for their daughters." Further, the Prophet asked, "Would you like it for your sister?" The Prophet received the same answer and made the same comment. The Prophet went on asking about the man's paternal and maternal aunts. The young man's answer was the same and the Prophet repeated the same comment, "People do not like that for their aunts." The Prophet then placed his hand on the young man and prayed for him, "O Allah, forgive his sins, purify his heart, and protect his chastity." (Al Albani)

Questions

- What is pornography?
- What is masturbation?
- Why do people look at pornography and masturbate?
- Why is looking at pornography and masturbating Haram?
- What should we remember if we feel like looking at pornography and masturbating, to help us control our Nafs and fight against the whispers of Shaitan?

Activities

- Watch a documentary about the experience of men and women who have worked in the pornography industry
- Watch a documentary about addiction to pornography and how it has affected people's lives
- Make a firm intention with Allah as your witness that you will not be ungrateful for the blessing that is your eyes by using them to look at pornography, and ask Him in exchange to bless you with seeing the Prophet (peace be upon him) in your dreams
- Make a firm intention with Allah as your witness that you will not masturbate, and ask Him in exchange to bless you with a beautiful spouse and pious children

4. PHYSICAL AND MENTAL HEALTH IN ISLAM

4.1

Male and Female Circumcision

Objectives

- To understand why Muslim males are circumcised
- To explore the history of female circumcision
- To consider why some people believe male circumcision is child abuse

Keywords

- Circumcision
- Foreskin
- Fitra
- FGM

What is male circumcision and why do we do it?

Male circumcision is the surgical removal of the foreskin. In Arabic this is called Khitan (referring to the procedure and also the name given to foreskin). It is not directly mentioned in the Qur'an, but the Prophet Muhammad told us that when the Prophet Ibrahim (peace be upon them both) was 80 years old he circumcised himself as per the command of Allah. This is why male circumcision is practiced by the Jews. There are several verses of the Qur'an in which Allah tells us to follow the example of the Prophet Ibrahim (peace be upon him), who was a sincere worshipper of the one true God, Allah.

The Prophet (peace be upon him) said: "Ibrahim (peace be upon him) circumcised himself when he was eighty years old..." (Bukhari)

We revealed to you: "Follow Ibrahim's religion, the pure in faith... (Qur'an 16:123)

There are reports that either the Prophet Muhammad (peace be upon him) was born without a foreskin or that his grandfather circumcised him when he was a baby. In a Hadith he told us that male circumcision is a part of Fitra, along with removing the pubic and underarm hair, trimming the moustache, and cutting the nails. Fitra is the natural state in which Allah has created us, which is one of purity and goodness. In the context of this Hadith, what the Prophet (peace be upon him) is telling us is that by doing these five things we are acting according to the Fitra.

Narrated Syedina Abu Hurayrah (may Allah be pleased with him): "I heard the Prophet (peace be upon him) saying: 'Five practices are characteristics of the Fitra: circumcision, shaving the pubic hair, cutting the moustache short, clipping the nails, and depilating the hair of the armpits.'" (Bukhari)

The Prophet (peace be upon him) circumcised his grandsons, Syedina Hassan and Hussain (may Allah be pleased with them both) when they were seven days old.

Why is the procedure carried out in infancy?

Within the different Islamic sects and schools of law there are different opinions about whether male circumcision is compulsory, or not compulsory but highly recommended. There is no specific ruling regarding the age at which circumcision should take place but in general it should be before puberty. Many people choose to get their sons circumcised as infants to follow the example set by the Prophet (peace be upon him) and because it is easier to have done as a baby compared to when you're older, and it will heal quicker.

Following the commands of our Creator

Why has Allah made circumcision part of being a Muslim boy/man? As Muslims we believe that each and every one of Allah's commands and prohibitions contain many wisdoms. For some things, Allah has told us, for others Islamic scholars have been able to work it out. However, for other things we might not know, or it might even seem paradoxical. Allah might have prohibited us from something we want to do, or He might have given us an order we do not want carry out. If we believe that Allah is our Lord and Creator, the One who is omniscient, then it shouldn't matter to us whether we can understand the wisdom behind His commands and prohibitions, we should obey without question or hesitation.

If we don't do this, if we feel the need to be able to understand something otherwise we are not willing to do it, then we are like the Shaitan. When Allah created the Prophet Adam (peace be upon him) and told all the Angels and Iblis to bow down to him, Iblis refused because to him it didn't make any sense. He argued with Allah that he was better than the Prophet Adam (peace be upon him), who was made of clay, because he was made of fire.

"What stopped you from prostrating when I commanded you?" said Allah, he (Iblis) replied, "I am better than him since You created me from fire, and him from clay." (Qur'an 7:12)

He should have realised that even though he couldn't understand the wisdom behind Allah's command, he should still have followed it. So the main reason why Muslim boys get circumcised is because it is the command of Allah and the example of His Prophet (peace be upon him).

Health benefits

In recent years medical researchers have found that being circumcised has some health benefits. This includes having less urinary tract infections, less risk of sexually transmitted diseases (including HIV), protection against penile cancer, and reduced risk of cervical cancer for their future wife. In general, all of these health benefits are because the foreskin traps dirt, bacteria and viruses, and makes it more difficult to keep the head of the penis clean. This is why the Prophet (peace be upon him) included male circumcision with other acts associated with good hygiene.

Circumcision, as long as it is done using clean instruments and by people who are properly trained, and the wound is taken care of after procedure to prevent infection, does not harm the penis. The circumcised penis does not function any differently than an uncircumcised penis, such as passing urine or having sex.

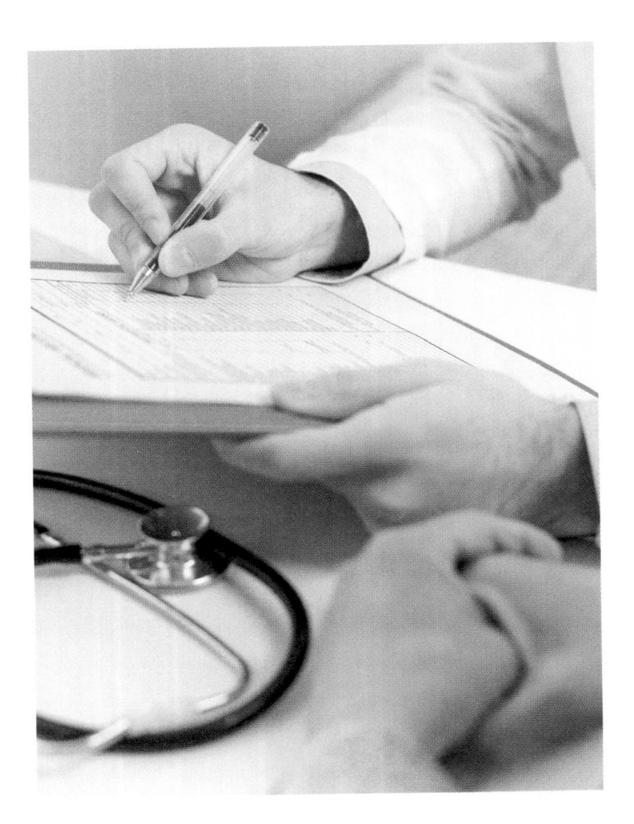

However, there are certain circumstances when a boy should not be circumcised. If a baby is born with hypospadias (where the hole through which urine exits the body is not at the tip of the head of the penis), surgeons can need to use the foreskin to correct the disorder and so parents are advised not to get their son circumcised.

Is it child abuse?

Some people argue that parents shouldn't get their sons circumcised when they are babies because the child is not being allowed to make up their own mind and when they are older they may wish they weren't circumcised. Therefore, they claim that male circumcision is a form of child abuse. However, based on this principle, piercing a baby girl's ears also constitutes child abuse, since we are performing a painful and permanent procedure for which she has not given consent due to her age, and may regret having later in life.

Furthermore, given nearly all male Muslims are circumcised, including many who convert to the faith as teenagers or adults, it is more likely a Muslim child would wish his parents had got him circumcised as a baby rather than leaving it until he is older and able to ask for it. During childhood the uncircumcised child would feel different and left out in their own community, and might be teased and bullied by other Muslim children. Therefore, you could argue that Muslim parents who do not have their sons circumcised in infancy are guilty of knowingly exposing their child to emotional abuse. As a teenager or adult, to fit in and fulfil a requirement of their faith they now have to go through a sensitive and painful procedure, whereas if it was carried out when they were a baby they wouldn't even remember having it done. Therefore, as Muslims, we strongly believe that male circumcision is not a form of child abuse, and parents are acting in what they perceive to be the best interests of their child.

What is female circumcision?

Female circumcision (also called female genital mutilation - FGM) describes different procedures, from removal of the clitoral hood and shortening of the inner labia (cosmetic surgical procedures called hoodectomy and labiaplasty, which many women, irrespective of religion or culture have done because they believe it makes their genitals more attractive), all the way

the clitoris, inner and outer labia, and closing the vulva, leaving a small hole for passage of urine and menstrual blood (a surgical procedure called infibulation, also known as pharaonic circumcision).

Female circumcision/FGM has been practiced in many different parts of the world for thousands of years, including the ancient Egyptians and ancient Greeks. It was done in childhood with the intention of decreasing female sexual desire, to make it less likely for girls to commit fornication. Even in the 19th century in the UK and US, doctors would perform a procedure to remove or reduce the size of the clitoris for the same reasons.

Is FGM beneficial or harmful?

FGM, especially the more severe forms and especially if carried out with instruments that are not sterile and by people who are not trained surgeons, has no proven benefit but can cause many problems. During the procedure children can die due to excessive blood loss, or shortly afterwards due to severe wound infection. Given the sensitivity of the body parts involved the procedure itself is extremely painful, and recovery can take a long time.

Girls can experience problems with not being able to pass urine, or with passage of blood during their menstrual period because the hole that is left is too small. Once married, having sex can be very painful. Scar tissue due to infections related to the procedure can cause problems with fertility, and during childbirth.

However, in cultures where FGM is widely practiced (e.g. some parts of the Middle East and Africa), it is a social norm, and if a girl has not had it done, her family would not be able to find her a husband. In these societies, FGM is promoted by women who were themselves circumcised during childhood.

Does Islam tell us to carry out female circumcision?

The position supporting female circumcision

The traditional Islamic position is that female circumcision is allowed, and even desirable. This is based on several Hadith. Once the Prophet (peace be upon him) met a woman who performed female circumcision and prohibited her from cutting too much.

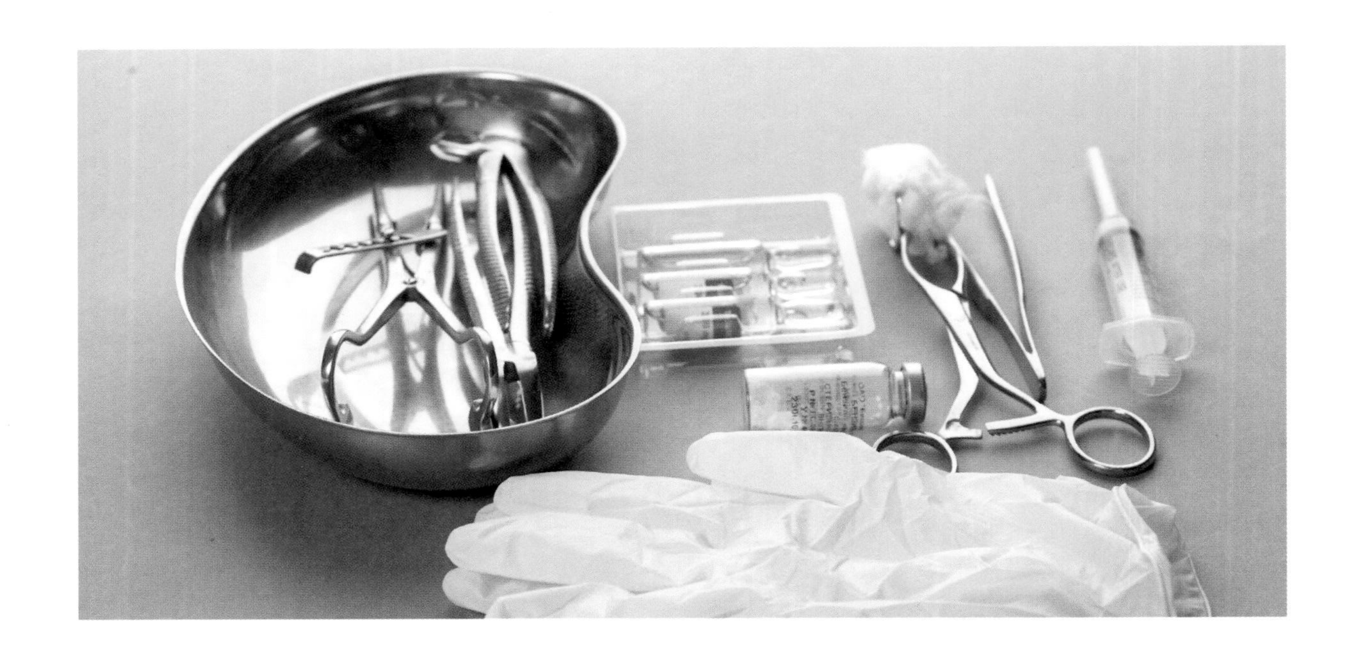

Narrated Syedatuna Umm 'Atiyyah al-Ansariyyah (may Allah be pleased with her) that a woman used to do circumcisions in Madinah and the Prophet (peace be upon him) said to her: "Do not go to the extreme in cutting; that is better for the woman and more liked by the husband." (Abu Dawood)

In another Hadith the Prophet (peace be upon him) said that circumcision is a Sunnah for men and an honour for women.

The Prophet (peace be upon him) said: "Circumcision is an act of Sunnah for men and an honourable act for women." (Ahmad)

In a third Hadith the Prophet told us that when two circumcised parts touch (i.e. sexual intercourse takes place), it becomes mandatory to perform Ghusl (full body ritual purification, i.e. to have a bath/shower).

The Prophet (peace be upon him) said: "When a man sits between the four parts (arms and legs of his wife) and the two circumcised parts meet, then Ghusl is obligatory." (Muslim)

The other Hadith used to support female circumcision was quoted earlier regarding it being part of Fitra. Many scholars have understood this to apply to both boys and girls.

The importance of differentiating female circumcision from FGM

According to the Human Rights Watch organisation, 85% of FGM cases worldwide involve partial or total removal of the clitoris, and can involve removal of the inner and outer labia. In a much smaller proportion of cases infibulation or pharaonic circumcision is performed. However, Islamic scholars who support female circumcision have pointed out that these procedures are too extreme, and exactly what the Prophet was advising against in the above Hadith. They argue that female circumcision should just involve hoodectomy (where the 'covering' of the clitoris is being reduced in size or removed, similar to how the covering of the head of the penis, the foreskin, is removed in male circumcision) and/or labiaplasty (where a large inner labium is reduced in size). It should be done for the same reason male circumcision is carried out, as an act of obedience to our Creator, not because of concerns regarding girls being able to control their sexual desires.

Other scholars have gone further to say that every female child should be reviewed by a doctor, and only if they have a prominent clitoral hood or large inner labia should the procedure be carried out to reduce their size, otherwise there is no need. In all cases, the procedure should carried out using sterile equipment and by a trained surgeon.

The position opposing female circumcision

There are other Islamic scholars who go even further, and argue that even these forms of female circumcision are not part of Islam. They argue that the Hadith used to support the practice are either Da'if (weak) because there are problems in the Sanad (the chain of transmitters going back to the Prophet) and therefore, cannot be used to create legal rulings, or can be interpreted to be referring to just male circumcision based on their understanding of the exact Arabic wording.

Furthermore, they argue that if female circumcision was a widespread practice during the time of the Prophet (peace be upon him) we would have many Hadith related to it, and accounts from the wives and daughters of the Prophet (peace be upon him), and his companions (may Allah be pleased with them all) regarding this. Someone might argue that such a private thing would not be publicly discussed and that is why we lack many Hadith, but this is not the case for other private matters which the Prophet and his wives have very clearly explained (such as related to sexual matters, menstruation, and cleaning yourself after going to the toilet).

They conclude that female circumcision was not a part of Islam and if it was practised during the lifetime of the Prophet (peace be upon him), it was likely a practise already present among the Arabs. It has continued as a cultural, rather than religious practice, as evidenced by the fact that according to a UNICEF report from 2013, there were 17 African countries in which at least 10% of Christian women had undergone FGM (with a rate as high as 55% in Niger). In some of these (e.g. Kenya, Tanzania, Niger), the rates among Christians was higher than among Muslims.

A practical approach from an Islamic perspective

Therefore, there isn't currently a consensus position among scholars regarding the status of female circumcision in Islam. However, what they are agreed upon is that Islam does not promote female circumcision to help girls control their sexual desires and prevent them from committing fornication. Furthermore, when considering the harm that more severe forms of FGM can cause, there is consensus that these are prohibited. Islam promotes female sexuality (within marriage) and forbids harming our bodies.

The extent of difference between the scholarly positions is on whether female circumcision, involving at most hoodectomy and/or labiaplasty and carried out using sterile tools by a trained surgeon, is mandatory (with only one school of religious law claiming as such), optional, or not actually a part of Islam at all.

Given the significant and lifelong physical and psychological harm to millions of women that is caused by FGM as practiced in the world today, and that female circumcision is considered optional even by the majority of scholars who believe it is an Islamic practice, there is an argument to be made the Muslims should support the worldwide banning of this practice. In 2006 there was a conference on female circumcision/FGM at Al-Azhar University in Egypt, attended by scholars from around the world, of different schools of religious law and sects. They issued Fatwas against the practice as it is carried out in the world today. Therefore, Muslims in the UK should have no issue abiding by the current laws which makes illegal any cosmetic surgery to the female genitalia of a child, thereby including all forms of FGM.

Believers, obey Allah, the Messenger and those among you in authority... (Qur'an 4:59)

The Prophet (peace be upon him) said: "It is necessary upon a Muslim to listen to and obey the ruler, as long as one is not ordered to carry out a sin. If he is commanded to commit a sin, then there is no adherence and obedience." (Bukhari)

Conclusion

Allah has told us to carry out male circumcision, as He did to some of His greatest Prophets (peace be upon them all). Allah is our Lord and Creator, our lives and bodies are gifts from Him that we are entrusted with for a while until He takes them back. If we remember this then whether we understand the wisdom in His commands or not, we will be happy to carry them out. But recently, through advances in medical research, we have found out the health benefits of male circumcision which help us understand why the Prophet (peace be upon him) included it as part of our Fitra. The situation regarding female circumcision is more complex, with a disagreement between scholars as to whether it is an Islamic practice or not. However, they are all in agreement that what is practiced as female genital mutilation (FGM) in much of the world is prohibited in Islam due to its incorrect intention, and how extreme and harmful it is. In the UK the practice is illegal and Muslims should be happy to abide by that.

Questions

- What is Fitra?
- Why did the Prophet (peace be upon him) include male circumcision as part of Fitra?
- Why did Allah create the foreskin if He wanted us to remove it?
- Since when has FGM been practised, and why is it normally done?
- What problems can result from FGM?
- Does Islam tell us to perform female circumcision, if so, to what extent and for what purpose?
- What should be the Muslim response to the current UK laws regarding FGM, and why?

Activities

- Do some research regarding the health benefits associated with male circumcision
- Do some research regarding the ceremonies and celebrations people in different cultures and countries have when performing male circumcision
- Watch a documentary or read stories of women who have undergone FGM and how it has affected their lives

4.2

Contraception and Abortion

Objectives

- To understand the purpose of marriage in Islam
- To explore how different intentions and methods of contraception affect its permissibility
- To consider how Tawakkul can affect a couple's decision to use contraception or have an abortion

Keywords

- Contraception
- Abortion
- Qadr
- Tawakkul

The importance of marriage

Marriage is given great importance in Islam. By partaking in the legal and spiritual ceremony, a man and woman become husband and wife, and go from being Haram (impermissible) to Halal (permissible) for each other. In the Qur'an Allah reminds us what an immense blessing this is for us to reflect on and be grateful for.

Another of His signs is He created spouses for you from your own kind, in them you find comfort; and He nurtured love and kindness between you, in that are signs for the thinkers. (Qur'an 30:21)

An expression of this love is the sexual act. Islam promotes this within the confines of marriage:

Your women are like pastures for you, so enter your pastures as you wish... (Qur'an 2:223)

The Prophet (peace be upon him) said: "...Having intercourse (with one's wife) is a charity." His companions (may Allah be pleased with them all) said: "O Messenger of Allah, if one of us fulfils his desire, is there reward in that?" The Prophet (peace be upon him) said, "Do you not see that if he does it in a Haram way he will have the burden of sin? So if he does it in a Halal way, he will have a reward for that." (Muslim)

The purpose of marriage

When a couple have sexual intercourse there is the possibility the wife will become pregnant. This is the most important purpose of having sex since it is necessary for the continuation of the human race.

People, be mindful of your Lord, He created you from a single person and created his partner from him, and then from the pair He spread countless men and women throughout the world... (Qur'an 4:1)

In Islam, sex and therefore pregnancy is only allowed to take place in the confines of marriage. Therefore, a primary purpose of marriage is to have children. This was promoted by the Prophet (peace be upon him).

The Prophet (peace be upon him) said: "Marry those who are loving and fertile, for I will be proud of your great numbers before the other nations." (Al Albani)

However, this is not the sole purpose of having sex in Islam. The Prophet (peace be upon him) encouraged foreplay, i.e. for the husband and wife to enjoy the sexual experience and for it not to just be a means to an end.

The Prophet (peace be upon him) said: "One of you should not fulfil one's (sexual) need from one's wife like an animal, rather there should be between them foreplay of kissing and words." (Al Daylami)

The Prophet (peace be upon him) said: "Do not have intercourse with your wife right away. Wait until she is as sexually aroused as you are." The man asked, "O Messenger of Allah, what should I do [in order to achieve that?]" He (peace be upon him) replied, "Kiss her, touch her, and try to arouse her. If you notice that she is as ready [sexually] as you are, then engage in the intercourse." (Al Mughni)

This is also shown by the fact that even though having intercourse during menstruation is Haram, the Prophet still recommended other types of physical contact between husband and wife during this time.

The Prophet (peace be upon him) said: "Enjoy your wives (during their menses), but do not have intercourse." (Muslim)

What is contraception

Contraception is the deliberate attempt to prevent pregnancy from occurring as a consequence of sexual intercourse. Sex normally involves ejaculation of millions of sperm inside the vagina. The sperm swim through the cervix into the uterus and from there into the fallopian tubes. If the woman is ovulating an egg will have travelled from her ovaries into the fallopian tubes, where it can be fertilised (by a single sperm) and then has the potential to develop into a baby. The fertilised egg travels back into the uterus and implants into the wall of the uterus.

Interruption of this process at any stage will prevent pregnancy. For example, withdrawing the penis from the vagina before ejaculation occurs, or wearing a condom or diaphragm during intercourse will prevent sperm from reaching the egg. Oral contraceptive pills

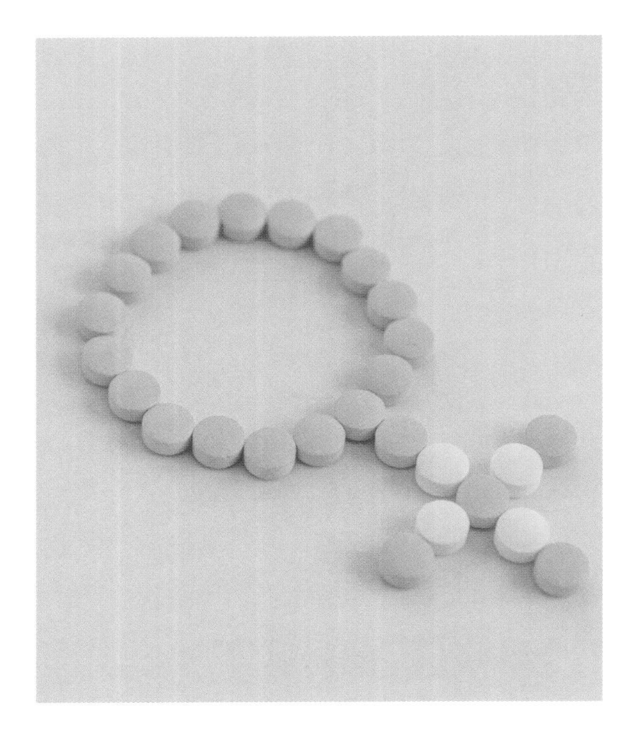

contain hormones which stop the ovaries from releasing eggs and the uterus from becoming ready for the fertilised egg to implant. Intrauterine devices (contraceptive devices placed within the uterus) such as the coil, prevent sperm from passing through the cervix and fertilised eggs from implanting into the uterine wall. These are all examples of reversible methods of contraception. Irreversible methods (surgical sterilisation) include vasectomy (an operation to cut the tube through which sperm leaves the testicles) and blocking or removal of the fallopian tubes.

Is contraception allowed in Islam?

With regards to the basic principle, contraception is allowed in Islam based on a Hadith in which a companion of the Prophet (may Allah be pleased with him) says that the Prophet (peace be upon him) was aware they practiced Azl (withdrawing the penis from the vagina prior to ejaculation) and did not prohibit it.

Syedina Jabir (may Allah be pleased with him) reported: "We used to practise Azl during the lifetime of Allah's Messenger (peace be upon him). This (the news of this practise) reached Allah's Prophet (peace be upon him), and he did not forbid us." (Muslim)

However, using other Islamic principles scholars have delved deeper to clarify what intentions or methods of contraception this would apply to.

It is important to consider intention when deciding on the permissibility of an action, as per the Hadith of the Prophet (peace be upon him) in which he said actions will be judged according to their intentions.

The Prophet (peace be upon him) said: "Actions are (judged) by motives (Niyyah), so each man will have what he intended. Thus, he whose migration (Hijrah) was to Allah and His Messenger, his migration is to Allah and His Messenger; but he whose migration was for some worldly thing he might gain, or for a wife he might marry, his migration is to that for which he migrated." (Bukhari)

In another Hadith we learn that having the intention to perform a good deed, even if we do not go on to perform it, will still earn us a reward, as will abstaining from a sin we had intended to partake in due to the remembrance of Allah.

The Prophet (peace be upon him) said: "Allah says to the Angels: 'If my servant intends a bad deed, do not record it unless he does it. If he does it, record it as one bad deed. If he leaves it for my sake, record for him one good deed. If he intends to do a good deed and he does not do it, record for him one good deed. If he does it, record for him ten good deeds like it up to seven-hundred times as much.'" (Bukhari)

Permissibility of different intentions for using contraception

Although there are differences in opinion between the schools of religious law and Islamic sects, there is a consensus that contraception is allowed if repeated pregnancies would harm the health of the mother or negatively impact the upbringing and care of previous children (especially with regards to their religious education and faith). According to some scholars this can include the need for a woman to work to provide for her family if her husband's earnings are not sufficient to meet their basic needs. However, if the husband's earnings are sufficient, then contraception for the purposes of career progression is generally not considered a valid reason.

There is also a scholarly consensus that both husband and wife must agree on the use of contraception, it should not be the decision of either one or the other without their spouse's knowledge or agreement. This is because having a child is a right of both partners in a marriage, which one of them should not deprive the other of.

Also, by consensus opinion using contraception for fear of poverty if you were to have more children is

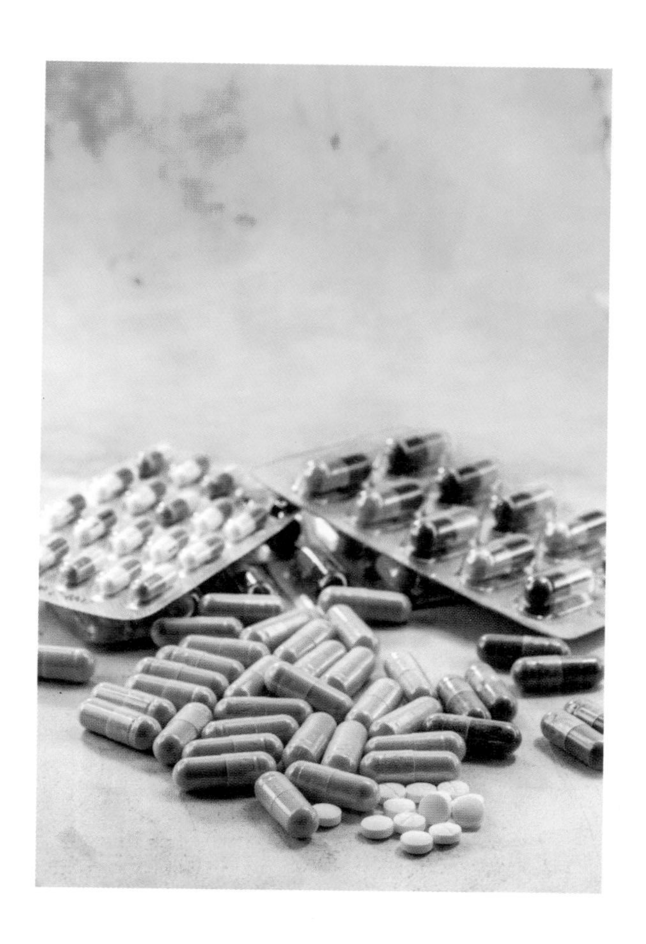

is impermissible. This is because it goes against the principle of relying on Allah as the provider of sustenance, as He clearly states in the Qur'an.

You shall not kill your children out of fear of poverty. We shall feed them and you; to kill them is a major sin and crime. (Qur'an 17:31)

There is a difference of scholarly opinion as to whether using contraception to space out pregnancies to allow a mother to get her figure back and maintain her beauty is permissible. Some argue that if there is the risk that her husband will find her less attractive and this will negatively impact their marriage and family, then it is permissible. Similarly, if husband and wife are going through serious marital difficulties some scholars have argued that using contraception is permissible if a further pregnancy could cause further strain on the marriage leading to divorce.

Permissibility of different methods of contraception

Irreversible methods of contraception (i.e. surgical sterilisation) are not allowed. This principle is taken from Hadith in which the Prophet (peace be upon him) forbade his companions from castrating themselves, and the Qur'anic verses quoted above from which we understand that having children is a primary purpose of marriage and sex.

Syedina Abdullah ibn Masood (may Allah be pleased with him) said: "We were on a campaign with the Messenger of Allah (peace be upon him), and we had no women with us. We said: 'Why don't we get ourselves castrated?' But he forbade us to do that." (Bukhari)

The exception is for medical purposes, e.g. if the mother's life would be in danger if she became pregnant again.

Methods of reversible contraception that involve inserting something into the vagina, e.g. female condom, diaphragm, intrauterine coil, are considered permissible but disliked by some schools of religious law.

The principle of not causing harm to yourself must also be considered. Some women lose a lot of blood due to heavier and longer periods while using the copper coil. Given there are alternatives and contraception is not mandatory in the first place, this would make it impermissible for them to use the copper coil. Regarding hormonal contraceptives, they are not meant to be used by women who have certain health conditions. Research has also shown that with long term use they increased the risk of breast and cervical cancer, while reducing the risk of endometrial, ovarian and colorectal cancer. A Muslim must take all of these factors into account.

Qadr – the Divine Decree

In many Hadith regarding Azl (the withdrawal method of contraception), while the Prophet (peace be upon him) didn't prohibit its use, he did remark that it makes no difference because if Allah has willed for you to have a child, it will happen regardless.

The Prophet (peace be upon him) said: "...It does not matter if you do not do it (Azl), for every soul that is to be born up to the Day of Resurrection will be born."

So, is the Prophet telling us to not bother using contraception because if pregnancy is going to result as a

consequence of intercourse it will happen regardless of whatever we do?

The Prophet (peace be upon him) was talking about a basic Islamic principle; Qadr, or the Divine Decree. As Muslims, we believe that nothing can happen without the will of Allah and through His power. His omniscience is such that even before the creation of the Universe, everything that is to ever happen was recorded in al-Lawh al-Mahfuz (the Preserved Tablet).

Any disaster on Earth or to yourselves is written down before it happens; this is easy for Allah. (Qur'an 57:22)

And with Him are the keys of the Unseen. None knows them but He; and He knows what is on land and sea; no leaf falls but that He knows it, nor any seed in the dark recesses of the earth, nor anything moist or dry, but that it is in a clear Book. (Qur'an 6:59)

The Prophet (peace be upon him) said, "...Know that even if the nation (or the whole community) were to gather together to benefit you with something, they would not benefit you with anything except that which Allah has already recorded for you, and that if they gather together to harm you with something, they would not be able to harm you with anything except that which Allah has already recorded against you. The pens have been lifted and the pages have dried." (Tirmidhi)

Therefore, it would be absurd to think that anything, such as contraception for example, is working against the Divine Decree; that is impossible. Indeed, everything is encompassed within Allah's infinite knowledge and power. This means that whether or not we use contraception, and whether or not a pregnancy occurs with or without the use of contraception, this is all part of the Divine Decree.

But this does not mean we refuse to use contraception, even if there is a valid reason for doing so (e.g. the mother's life will be in danger if she becomes pregnant) due to an incorrect belief that if Allah has willed for a pregnancy to occur, it will happen regardless of what we do. This is no different from a couple wishing to become pregnant but not having sex because if Allah wills for them to have a child, it will happen regardless. Allah has created the Universe with natural laws that follow cause and effect. And the Prophet (peace be upon him) taught us to act according to our knowledge and ability, but also rely on Allah; e.g. when the Prophet (peace be upon him) went to war, he prayed to Allah to give the Muslims victory and he wore two sets of armour.

A man said, "O Messenger of Allah, should I tie my camel and trust in Allah, or should I leave her untied and trust in Allah?" The Prophet (peace be upon him) said, "Tie her and trust in Allah." (Tirmidhi)

Some couples try to have children for decades without any success, whereas there are cases (although very rare) of couples where either the husband or wife has undergone surgical sterilisation, but a pregnancy has still resulted.

Therefore, when a Muslim couple use contraception with an aim to avoid pregnancy, they must do so realising that ultimately whether the wife ends up becoming pregnant or not is in accordance with the Divine Decree, i.e. up to Allah.

Tawakkul – trust and reliance on Allah

As Muslims, Tawakkul (having trust and reliance on Allah) is an important part of our faith. We might have valid reasons for wanting to

avoid a pregnancy, however these are based on our limited knowledge and predictions for the unknown future. But Allah is omniscient, He knows everything and since He is outside of time (it is one of His creations and under His command), for Him there is no past, present or future.

So, we might not want something believing it would be worse for us, but Allah knows that it would be better for us. For example, we might believe a further pregnancy would have a negative impact on the mother's health, or ability of the parents to look after previous children. However, with the new child our life might change in other ways such as getting a job promotion, or the relationship between husband and wife improving, creating a better home environment for everyone.

Furthermore, even in hardship there can be immense benefit. This life is a test, and sometimes this takes the form of difficulty and sorrow. For example, if a couple were to have a disabled child but took care of him or her to the best of their ability, with patience and while still expressing gratitude to Allah, this would please Him and could be the means by which they become of the Awliyah Allah.

"...sometimes you may dislike something that is good for you, and sometimes you may like something that is bad for you. Only Allah knows the whole truth, not you." (Quran 2:216)

Syedina Umar Ibn al-Khattab (may Allah be pleased with him) relates that some prisoners were brought before Allah's Messenger (peace be upon him) and amongst them was a woman who was frantically searching for someone in the crowd. When she found a baby amongst the prisoners, she took it in her arms, cradled it next to her chest and suckled it. So Allah's Messenger (peace be upon him) said: "Do you think that this woman would ever throw her

child into the fire?" We said: 'By Allah, never!' So he said: "Allah is more merciful to His believing servants than that mother could ever be to her child." (Bukhari)

"How wonderful is the affair of the believer, for his affairs are all good, and this applies to no one but the believer. If something good happens to him, he is thankful for it and that is good for him. If something bad happens to him, he bears it with patience and that is good for him." (Muslim)

"Whatever Allah has decreed for His believing slave is a blessing, even if that is in the form of withholding; it is a favour even if that is in the form of a trial; and the calamity decreed by Him is fair, even if it us painful." (Madaarij al-Saalikeen)

Do people think they will be left alone once they've declared, "We believe," then will not be tested? We tested those before them. Allah knows the truthful and the liars. (Qur'an 29:2-3)

The Prophet (peace be upon him) said: "When a person's child dies, Allah the Most High asks His Angels, 'Have you taken the life of the child of My slave?' They reply in the affirmative. Allah then asks them, 'Have you taken the fruit of his heart?' They reply in the affirmative. Thereupon He asks, 'What has My slave said?' The Angels say, 'He praised you and said 'Inna lillahi wa inna ilayhi raji'oon (To Allah we belong and to Him we will return). 'At that Allah replies, 'Build a home for my slave in Jannah and call it 'Bayt-ul-Hamd' (Home of Praise).'" (Tirmidhi)

This is not to say we do not follow medical advice, or just focus on having as many children as possible without giving any regard to our ability to give them a good upbringing. However, once we have acted according to the extent of our knowledge and with the best of intentions, we must remember that whatever happens, whatever the result is, is according to the Divine Decree and we must have Tawakkul; trust and reliance in Allah that it will be better for us.

What is abortion?

As the foetus (unborn child) develops in the womb of the mother, it reaches a stage around 22 to 23 weeks after conception (fertilisation of the egg) when, if born early it might be able to survive (with intensive medical care). If birth occurs prior to 22 weeks, the premature baby would not be able to survive. This is called spontaneous abortion, or late miscarriage.

Induced abortion is a medical process of ending or terminating a pregnancy so it doesn't result in the birth of a live baby. This can be done via medication (causing the womb to expel the foetus), or surgery (to remove the contents of the womb).

Is abortion allowed in Islam?

The Prophet (peace be upon him) said there are three stages of development following conception, each spanning 40 days, following which an Angel breathes the spirit or soul into the body.

The Prophet (peace be upon him) said: "Verily the creation of each one of you is brought together in the mother's belly for forty days in the form of a seed, then he is a clot of blood for a like period, then a morsel of flesh for a like period, then there is sent to him the Angel who blows the breath of life into him..." (Bukhari)

This is mirrored by the Qur'an, in which Allah tells us the different stages of foetal development before it develops into another form of creation, which according to Qur'anic scholars is reference to ensoulment (the soul/spirit entering the body).

...We placed him as a drop of semen in the stable environment of the womb. The drop of semen turned to a bloodlike clot; and, from the bloodlike clot, We created a fleshy lump; and then We made bones and covered them with flesh; then We produce from it another created form. (Qur'an 23:13-14)

Therefore, when the foetus reaches 120 days of development (roughly 4 months, or 17 weeks), it is classified classified as a human being (since it has both body and soul) and it is impermissible to have an abortion since this is tantamount to murder.

You shall not kill your children out of fear of poverty. We shall feed them and you; to kill them is a major sin and crime. (Qur'an 17:31)

...whoever kills another person – unless it is in lawful retaliation for taking a life or for wreaking havoc throughout the land – it is as though he has killed the whole of humanity... (Qur'an 5:32)

The only exception is if continuing pregnancy would put the mother's life in danger. In these cases, applying the principle of the lesser of two evils and that certainty should not be overridden by doubt (because the baby might live, but the mother is definitely alive), the foetus can be aborted.

There is less agreement among scholars from different schools of religious law and Islamic sects regarding abortion prior to 120 days. On the one extreme, some argue that once the egg has been fertilised it has the potential to become a human being and therefore taking any action that stops this is impermissible. On the other extreme some argue that abortion is allowed (but disliked) up to 120 days because until the soul is breathed into it, it cannot be considered a human being (despite its potential) and may be thought of as an extension of the mother's body.

The more widespread view falls in between these extremes. It is that because of the value of even a potential human life, abortion (even up to 120 days) should only be considered in specific cases, and even then, as a disliked act. This includes harm to the mother's health if pregnancy continues, pregnancy due to rape, or extreme foetal deformity which means the baby would either not survive following birth or have no quality of life (i.e. would lack the ability to function as a human being). In such circumstances, the earlier the abortion is carried out the better, and it should be with consent from both husband and wife.

The Islamic principles of Qadr and Tawakkul (as discussed previously in relation to contraception), should also be considered.

Conclusion

Islam promotes a healthy sex life within the confines of marriage. While the primary purpose of this is to have children, this is not the sole purpose and as such, contraception is allowed. Similarly, with regards to abortion, Islam recognises that there are certain circumstances in which this disliked act is a necessity. Islam places huge value on even the potential of human life, and so these decisions must not be taken lightly, or for frivolous reasons. We must remember that this life is a test, and this will take the form of hardship at times. The patience we exhibit and the gratitude to Allah for His immeasurable blessings upon us, even within the difficulties we face, will determine the outcome of our test. What we are offered is no less than an eternity in Paradise and the pleasure of our Creator.

Questions

- What is the primary purpose of marriage and sex in Islam?
- Is this the only purpose?
- What is contraception?
- Is contraception allowed in Islam?
- What types, and in what circumstances is contraception not allowed?
- What is abortion?
- Is abortion allowed in Islam, and why?
- What are the different views of Islamic schools of law and sects on this topic?

Activities

- Do some research on the different types of contraception used by people in the past
- Do some research on the different types of contraception available today, and how they work
- Do some research on the different methods of abortion and when and why they are used
- Do some research regarding the UK law on abortion
- Read about or watch a documentary about women who have had an abortion, what their reasons for having it were, what their experience was like, and what they think about it now

4.3

Blood and Organ Donation

Objectives

- To understand why Islam promotes donation of blood
- To explore the arguments for and against organ donation in Islam
- To consider the daily life of someone with organ failure waiting for a transplant

Keywords

- Blood
- Organ
- Donate
- Transplant

Why might people need blood?

There are many medical conditions and emergencies in which patients can require a blood transfusion to help save their lives. They might have lost a lot of blood during an accident or operation. Their body might not produce enough new blood cells to replace old ones, or the blood cells it makes don't function as normal. A disease process might be causing their blood cells to be destroyed quicker than normal.

To have blood ready to give to people who need it, healthy people need to donate their blood. This involves making an appointment at a blood donation clinic where you complete a short questionnaire to check you are healthy. If that is OK, they give you about 500ml of water or juice to drink before they take roughly the same volume of blood (to maintain the amount of fluid in your circulation). Once the procedure is finished (the blood donation itself only takes less than 10 minutes) you can have a couple more drinks and a snack before going home.

Can Muslims donate blood?

There are relatively few Muslim blood donors because many of us aren't sure it is allowed in Islam. We might have concerns that Islam

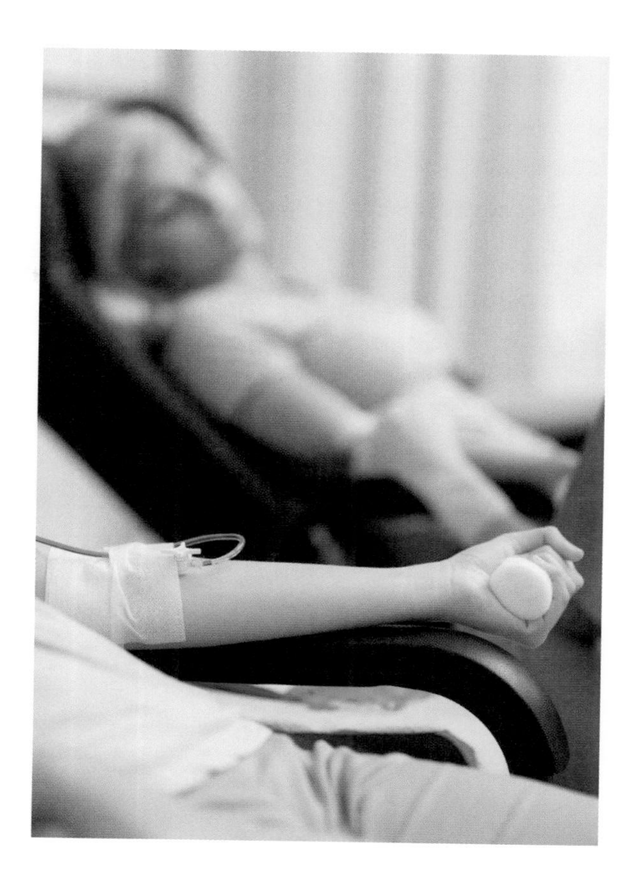

teaches us that we shouldn't harm our bodies. Also, how do we know who is going to receive the blood we donate? What if it is going to a non-Muslim, who because of the blood they receive, live longer and commit more sins? Would we be held responsible for that?

In the Qur'an Allah forbids Muslims from eating dead flesh, drinking blood, or eating pigs, but if someone is forced to, or is starving and has to to stay alive, then it is permissible.

You are forbidden to eat: carrion; blood; pork; whatever is slaughtered in a name other than Allah's...So anyone forced by famine to eat these forbidden meats, not out of perverse desire to sin, will find Allah Forgiving, Most Kind. (Qur'an 5:3)

This tells us the importance Allah gives to saving a life, in that the impermissible becomes permissible under those extreme circumstances. In the same way, if you were to insert a needle into your arm and draw out some blood for no reason this would be a sin, you would be harming your body without a good reason to do so. But if that blood is to help someone else who needs it, then this becomes a permissible and even praiseworthy act.

Allah also tells us in the Qur'an that He has not forbidden us from dealing in a just and kind manner with non-Muslims who are not our enemies.

Allah does not forbid you from being good and just to those who have not fought against you due to religion, nor expelled you from your houses... (Qur'an 60:8)

Therefore, it would even be allowed for a Muslim to directly donate blood to a non-Muslim, even though the way the service works in the UK, when we donate blood we don't know and can't find out who our blood will go to. This is similar in principle to how giving charity to non-Muslims is allowed and even recommended. Furthermore, in Islam we are not responsible for the actions of others so it doesn't matter if our blood helps a non-Muslim live longer and potentially commit more sins. Similarly, there is no prohibition on receiving the blood of a non-Muslim donor.

Giving your blood as an act of charity

Given the above, Islamic scholars are in agreement that blood donation is not only permissible but it is an act that earns the pleasure of Allah. This is because the purpose of donating blood is to help our fellow human being who is in great difficulty and may even need our blood to stay alive. Therefore, this is a similar act to saving someone who is drowning or trapped in a burning building. Allah tells us in the Qur'an that if anyone saves a life it is as if they saved the whole of humanity.

...whoever kills another person – unless it is in lawful retaliation for taking a life or for wreaking

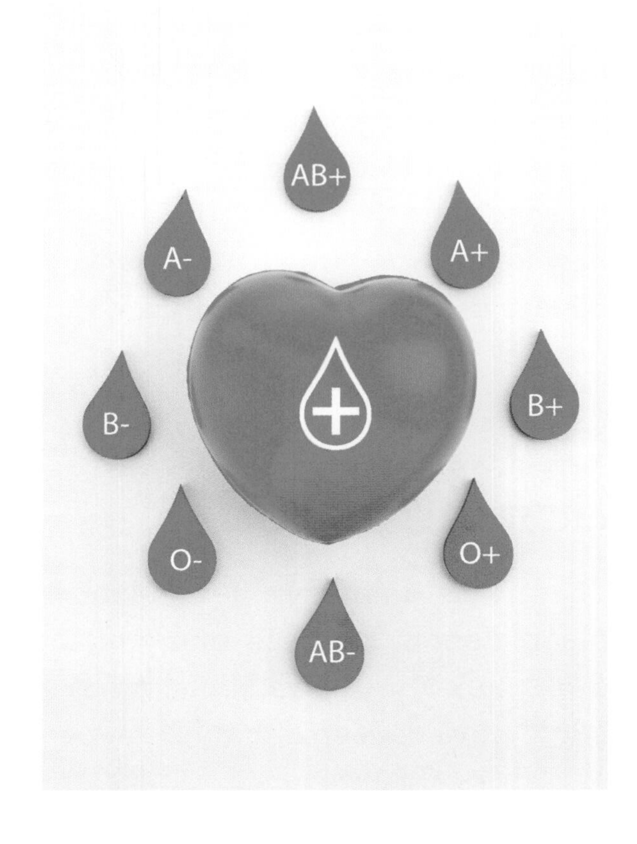

havoc throughout the land – it is as though he has killed the whole of humanity, and anyone who saves a life, it is as though he has saved the whole of humanity... (Qur'an 5:32)

Another way to think about it, is that in the same way we can give charity with our money, time, words and actions, donating our blood is another act of charity. Allah multiplies our charity by at least 700 times when He rewards us for it and the charity we give also helps to erase our sins, prevents calamities and cools Allah's anger for our misdeeds.

Those people who spend their wealth in Allah's way are like a grain that sprouts to produce seven ears, each ear containing a hundred seeds, and Allah can multiply it many times further for whomever He pleases. Allah is The Vast, The All Knowing. (Qur'an 2:261)

The Prophet (peace be upon him) said: "Charity finishes sins as water extinguishes fire." (Tirmidhi)

The Prophet (peace be upon him) said: "Give charity without delay, for it stands in the way of calamity." (Tirmidhi)

The Prophet (peace be upon him) said: "Charity cools the wrath of Allah and prevents a bad death." (Tirmidhi)

What are the different types of organ donations?

Organ donation can be of different types, including tissues, such as skin, tendons, bone, heart valves, corneas, and organs, such as our heart, lungs, kidney, liver, pancreas and small bowel. The donated organ can be used in the donor's own body (autotransplantation – for example, using a blood vessel from the leg for a cardiac bypass operation), or in someone else's body (homotransplantation – for example, donating a kidney which is transplanted in someone with renal failure on dialysis). If the donated organ is from a different species to the one it is transplanted into (for example a pig heart valve transplanted into a human patient), this is called xenotransplantation. Donations can be from living or dead donors (who consented while alive or their family have agreed to organ donation after their death).

Someone is dead when their brain has stopped working permanently, or their heart and lungs have stopped working permanently.

Humans are a special creation of Allah

Muslims believe that humans are the most special creation of Allah. This is evident in the story of the Prophet Adam (peace be upon him) in which Allah created his body with His hands before blowing His spirit into him.

Remember when Your Lord told the Angels: "I am creating a representative on Earth." They replied: "Why are You creating someone who will make trouble there and shed blood? Is it not enough that we glorify You with praises and proclaim Your Holiness?" He said: "I know what you don't know." (Qur'an 2:30)

Remember when Your Lord said to Angels, "I am creating a human with dried clay from dark mud. Once I have shaped and blown My spirit into him, then prostrate before him." So all the Angels prostrated, except Iblis, who refused to prostrate. (Qur'an 15:28-31)

Allah said, "Iblis, what stopped you from prostrating to the creation of My Hands?... (Qur'an 38:75)

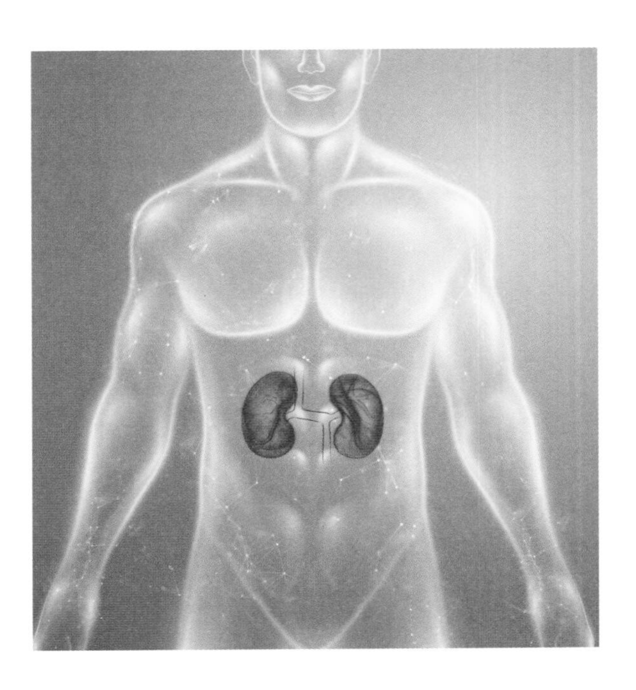

Furthermore, Allah says He has honoured the children of Adam (peace be upon him) and preferred them over His other creations. In fact, Allah tells us that the rest of creation is there for our use, and He has showered blessings upon us, both hidden and open. He tells us we have been created with the best form, which scholars say relates to how our physical appearance and our intellectual abilities are so much more beautiful and advanced compared to animals.

We created man in the most beautiful form. (Qur'an 95:4)

We honoured the children of Adam...and favoured them above all Our creation. (Qur'an 17:70)

Haven't you considered how Allah made everything in the Heavens and the Earth serve your needs, and bestowed His gifts on you, visible and hidden?... (Qur'an 31:20)

So, Islam teaches us that the human body is special and needs to be treated with respect, honour and dignity, irrespective of physical or spiritual differences.

Sydeina Sahl ibn Hunayf (may Allah be pleased with him) said: "A funeral procession passed by the Messenger of Allah (peace be upon him) so he stood up. We said, "It is the funeral procession of a Jew." He (peace be upon him) said: "Is it not a soul?" (Bukhari)

Respecting the dignity of the alive and the dead

Therefore, any action which doesn't treat a human or the human body with respect and dignity, in life or death, is not allowed. The Prophet (peace be upon him) told us that breaking the bone of a dead person is like breaking the bone of a living person and he also prohibited us from mutilating bodies. Some Islamic scholars have argued that this means organ transplantation from a living or dead donor is not allowed, including autotransplantation. This is supported by the Islamic principle that harming one person to benefit another is not allowed.

The Prophet (peace be upon him) said: "Breaking the bone of one who is dead is like breaking it when he is alive." (Abu Dawood)

The Prophet (peace be upon him) said: "...do not mutilate (the dead) bodies..." (Muslim)

The value of saving a life

Other scholars have argued that Hadith relating to mutilation and the breaking of bones were in relation to the damage being done to the dead person with a bad intention, i.e. to harm their bodies. This does not apply to organ transplantation, where skin and bones might be cut or sawn through to extract organs, but the body is treated with the utmost respect and the operation is being done for the purpose of saving the life or lives of the recipients of these organs.

The Prophet (peace be upon him) said: "Verily actions are by intentions, and for every person is what he intended..." (Bukhari)

...anyone who saves a life, it is as though he has saved the whole of humanity... (Qur'an 5:32)

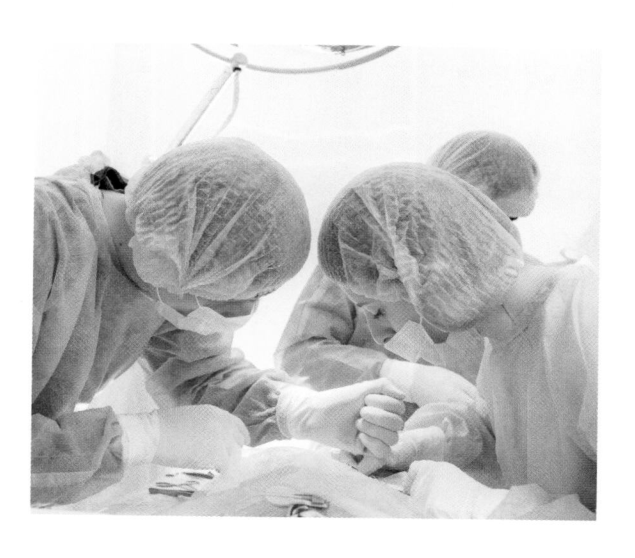

In today's society performing an operation on a dead body to remove organs does not degrade the dead body. In fact, it is considered one of the most praiseworthy acts a person can do and is a way of dignifying the dead person.

The lesser of two evils

If a pregnant woman is giving birth but the delivery is not progressing and the unborn baby's life is at risk, Islamic scholars are in agreement that it is permissible for an operation (caesarean section) to be performed to save the life of the baby (thereby arguably mutilating and harming the body of the mother). Furthermore, if during delivery the mother passes away but the unborn baby is still alive, scholars have argued that it is still permissible to perform the operation to try and save the life of the unborn baby despite this involving cutting the dead woman's body. This is because this is the less harmful action compared to doing nothing, in which case the unborn baby will die as well.

Some scholars have used this example in their argument regarding the permissibility of organ transplantation due to similarities in the underlying principle. Organ transplantation is only being done in cases of severe need, for the purpose of saving life, and where there is no alternative. This takes

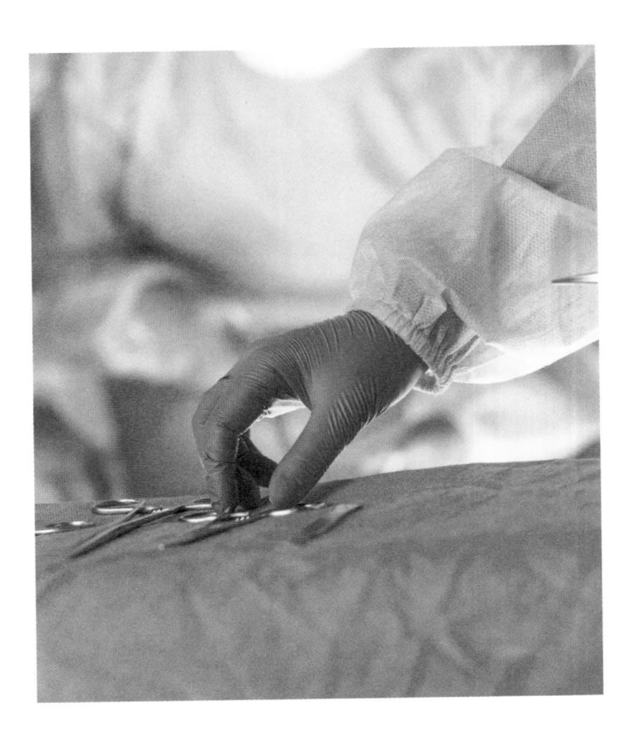

over protecting the dignity of a dead body, since saving a life is of greater importance. This is supported by the Islamic principles that necessity makes prohibition lawful and that we should choose the lesser of two evils.

However, even if we believe that organ transplantation is permissible, it would be forbidden to take an organ without the consent of the person whose body it is coming from, or their relatives if they have already passed away. So, for example, using organs of prisoners who are facing the death penalty would not be allowed unless they had consented of their own free will and not been coerced. Organs should also not be bought or sold since this would create a situation where the rich can benefit but the poor cannot, and some poor people would cause themselves harm by selling their organs for money.

Transplantation of animal tissues or organs

Regarding xenotransplantation (transplantation between members of different species) there is less difference in opinion between scholars, since this involves using part of an animal for human benefit. In the Qur'an Allah tells us He created animals for us to benefit from them, and the Prophet (peace be upon him) told us that we should use medicine to try and cure ourselves.

He created the livestock to provide wool for warmth, meat for you to eat, and they have other benefits too...They carry your loads from one city to another, without them you would travel with great difficulty. Your Lord is Compassionate and Kind. He created the horse, the mule and the donkey for you to ride... (Qur'an 16:5-8)

The Prophet (peace be upon him) said: "Treat sickness, for Allah has not created any disease except He has also created the cure..." (Tirmidhi)

Therefore, Islamic scholars argue that xenotransplantation from Halal animals is allowed. With regards to Haram animals, as previously discussed, in extreme circumstances Allah has given us permission to save our life by eating their flesh. This principle has been used to argue that in circumstances where there is no alternative and it can save a life, xenotransplantation is even allowed from Haram animals.

Conclusion

We should all become blood donors, it is a charitable act that will help save lives and gain Allah's pleasure. Regarding organ donation, although there are differences in opinion, especially regarding the permissibility of using organs from dead bodies for transplantation, many Islamic scholars from different schools of religious law and Islamic sects have accepted its permissibility and even promoted it as a charitable act (see recent UK Fatwa by Mufti Mohammed Zubair Butt - https://nhsbtdbe.blob.core.windows.net/umbraco-assets-corp/16300/organ-donation-fatwa.pdf).

Questions

- Why may people need a blood transfusion?
- Does giving blood cause harm to the donor?
- Are Muslims allowed to donate their blood?
- What are the different types of organ transplantation?
- What are the arguments against organ transplantation being allowed in Islam?
- What are the arguments for organ transplantation being allowed in Islam?

Activities

- Watch a documentary about people who need blood transfusions to save their lives
- Go to a blood donation clinic to see what happens there, and talk to some of the donors about why they donate their blood and how long they've been doing it for
- Watch a documentary about people who have organ failure and what their lives are like while they are on the transplantation waiting list
- Watch a recording of surgery carried out to harvest an organ from a dead body, and its transplantation into a patient

4.4

Vegetarianism

Objectives

- To understand that Islam allows for vegetarianism but also allows for eating meat
- To explore the impact on our health and the wider world of eating meat
- To consider whether the methods used by the meat industry comply with Islamic standards

Keywords

- Vegetarian
- Meat
- Abattoir
- Cruelty

Eating meat is allowed

Is it cruel to kill animals for meat, and if so why doesn't Islam teach us to be vegetarians? Every Prophet (peace be upon them all) was told by Allah what foods they and their community could and could not eat (i.e. what foods were Halal and Haram for them). As far as we know, from the Prophet Adam to the Prophet Muhammad (peace be upon them all), all of them were allowed to eat meat (with exceptions relating to specific animals). This means Allah, the One who created all the animals, and loves all of His creation more than we can imagine, has made it permissible for us to slaughter animals for the purpose of eating meat. Indeed, in the Qur'an Allah tells us this is one of the purposes with which He created animals.

He created the livestock to provide wool for warmth, meat for you to eat, and they have other benefits too...They carry your loads from one city to another, without them you would travel with great difficulty. Your Lord is Compassionate and Kind. He created the horse, the mule and the donkey for you to ride... (Qur'an 16:5-8)

For your benefit He created the sea; from it you get fresh meat to eat... (Qur'an 16:14)

Allah made for you homes to live in, and from the skins of animals you make tents that are light for you to carry about when travelling and camping, and from their wool, fur and hair you make furnishing that last for years. (Qur'an 16:80)

Do we have to eat meat?

However, just because eating meat is permissible, does not mean it is mandatory. It is allowed for a Muslim to be a vegetarian. In fact, if we look at the life of the Prophet (peace be upon him), many months would go by without his family eating cooked food. So even though he did eat meat, it would not be that often, and definitely not every day or even every week. This is also the case for most Muslims living in poorer countries, sometimes they might only have meat once a year on Eid-ul-Adha.

In this is a lesson for us, even if we eat meat it should not be too often. In wealthier countries most people eat too much meat and this is bad for their health (increasing their risk of developing certain cancers). Furthermore, a lot of plants and food is used to feed all the animals that are killed for us to be able to eat so much meat. If this food was instead given to starving people in poorer countries, many less people would die of hunger in the world.

Some people go further, to argue that at the time of the Prophet (peace be upon him), it would not have been possible for people to be healthy without including meat in their diet. But in modern times we can be vegetarian and as healthy, if not more, than people who eat meat. These people say that if the

(peace be upon him) was with us today he probably would have been a vegetarian, because he wouldn't want a single animal to lose its life if it didn't need to. He always taught his followers to be kind to animals.

The Prophet (peace be upon him) said: "There is a reward for kindness to every living animal..." (Bukhari)

The Prophet (peace be upon him) said: "Fear Allah in your treatment of animals." (Abu Dawood)

Syedina Abdullah ibn Mas'ud (may Allah be pleased with him) said: "We were once on a journey with the Messenger of Allah (peace be upon him) and he went off to answer the call of nature. We saw a Hummara (a small sparrow like

sparrow like bird) with two chicks and we took the two chicks. Then the Hummara came and began to flutter (around us). The Prophet (peace be upon him) came back and said, "Who has frightened this bird by (taking) its young? Give them back to her." (Abu Dawood)

The Prophet (peace be upon him) said: "Whoever kills a sparrow or anything bigger than that without a just cause, Allah will hold him accountable on the Day of Judgement." The listeners asked, "O Messenger of Allah, what is a just cause?" He replied, "That he will kill it to eat, not simply to chop off its head and then throw it away." (Al Nasai)

However, because Allah has allowed us to eat meat, and it was something the Prophet (peace be upon him) did and even enjoyed, we cannot say that eating meat is wrong, or should be Haram.

Syedina Abu Ubayd (may Allah be pleased with him) reports: "I cooked something for the Prophet in a saucepan. Since he liked the shoulder, I handed it to him. He then said to me: 'Give me the shoulder.' I said: 'Messenger of Allah, how many shoulders does a lamb have?' He said: 'By Him who holds my soul in His hand, had you complied, you would have given me as many shoulders as I would have asked for.'" (Ahmad)

How should we treat animals?

In Islam there are strict rules about how animals should be treated, especially when being slaughtered for food (the process, involving

its rules and regulations is called 'Dhabihah' in Arabic). Animals should always be treated with kindness and never made to suffer. This means they should not be kept in small cages or boxes, in too much heat or too much cold. They should be given good food to eat and enough water to drink. An animal shouldn't have to watch another animal being killed in front of it, in fact even the knife that is going to be used shouldn't be sharpened in front of it. To kill an animal, the knife should be extremely sharp, and while taking the name of Allah the throat is cut with one quick slice. This cuts through the big blood vessels between the heart and the brain. As a result, blood stops flowing to the brain and the animal immediately loses consciousness. Therefore, it can't feel any more pain after the first cut and it does not suffer even its body continues to jerk and move. Because the heart keeps pumping, this drains the body of blood (blood is Haram).

So eat of the meat on which Allah's name has been invoked... (Qur'an 6:118)

The Prophet (peace be upon him) cursed the one who did Muthla to an animal (i.e. cut its limbs or some other part of its body while it is still alive)." (Bukhari)

The Prophet (peace be upon him) said "If you must slaughter, slaughter in the best possible manner, sharpen your knife every time before you slaughter but not in front of the animal to be slaughtered. Do not slaughter an animal in the presence of other animals, and feed and rest the animal before slaughter." (Bukhari)

Conclusion

Even though we are allowed to eat meat in Islam we should not make it a daily habit, in fact we should try to eat it maybe once a week or less. This will be closer to the example of the Prophet (peace be upon him) and healthier for us. Islam does not prohibit us from becoming a vegetarian, but we should be careful not to think that we are better than other, meat-eating Muslims. If someone enquires as to us why we are a vegetarian Muslim, we can tell them our reasons and encourage them to also cut down on their meat intake. However, we should stop ourselves from telling others that they should also become a vegetarian, remembering that Allah has made it permissible and our Prophet (peace be upon him) enjoyed eating meat.

Questions

- Can a Muslim be a vegetarian?
- Why might some Muslims decide to become vegetarians?
- How often did the Prophet (peace be upon him) and early Muslims eat meat?
- What does Islam teach us about how we should treat animals who are going to be slaughtered for their meat?

Activities

- If you eat meat regularly, try and eat it less often
- Go to a farm and see how much food is used to grow animals that will be later killed for their meat
- Go to a Muslim abattoir and see how animals are killed for their meat according to the teachings of the Prophet (peace be upon him)

4.5

Coping with the Stress of Exams

Objectives

- To understand that exams are a necessary part of life for everyone and feeling stressed about them is normal
- To explore how we can reduce the stress we experience due to exams
- To consider what true success is and how we can learn from failure

Keywords

- Stress
- Exams
- Success
- Failure

Why do we have to do exams?

Doing exams is part of life, everyone has to do them. Exams enable us to show that we can apply what we have learnt and are ready to move onto something new, the next stage of our education. An exam can also be part of an application process for a school, university, or job. So no exam is meant to be impossible, if you do the work you are meant to do you should get a good result. To pass an exam you don't need to get all the questions right (although that should be your aim), you just have to make sure you don't get too many wrong.

Why exams are stressful

At the time in our life when we are preparing for an exam it can seem like the most important thing in the world. We can end up believing that the rest of our life (i.e. how successful we will be) depends on how well we do in this exam. This can make us very anxious. Some people find it so stressful that they become overwhelmed and feel unable to cope.

But once we get through the exam, in a year or two, we will probably have another set of exams. When this happens we realise the last exam was not that important or that difficult, this new exam is the really important and difficult one, and we start to get stressed again. This cycle repeats itself many times in our lives. By the end of our lives we will have done many, many exams.

One of the really stressful things about exams is that it all depends on how we do on the day, in the exam itself. We worry that we might not be able to work fast enough, or in our hurry we might not read the questions properly, or make too many silly mistakes and not get a chance to check our answers. We might face questions we don't know the answers to and start to panic.

How to feel less stressed

One method for reducing the likelihood of these things happening and to reduce our stress level is to get some exam practice. This can be by doing past questions and papers, in an exam like setting, either in school or at home. The more we do this the more used to doing exams we will get and so it will not be as stressful when it comes to the real thing. We will be used to working quickly, concentrating, avoiding silly mistakes or correcting them when we check our answers, and not panicking when we see difficult questions but trying our best to give good answers in the time we have.

Another way to feel less stressed is to remember that we can only do our best. As long as we have worked hard preparing for the exam and in the exam worked as quickly and carefully as we can, then whatever the result, whether we pass or fail, we should feel proud of ourselves that we have given it our 100% and could not have done any more.

Sometimes failure is meant to be

But even if the exam doesn't go as well as we hoped, even if we fail we should not become despondent and depressed. We should not think our life is over or that Allah is punishing us or didn't listen to our prayers.

Allah tells us in the Qur'an that He has written everything that will ever happen in Al-Lawh Al-Mahfooz (the Preserved Tablet) before we were even born, before the Universe was even created.

He has the keys of the unseen realm, only He knows them. He knows all that is in the land and the sea. Not a single leaf falls without His knowledge, no seed buried in the darkness of the earth, nor any fresh or withered plant is left unrecorded in a clear Book. (Qur'an 6:59)

"Any disaster on Earth or to yourselves is written down before it happens; this is easy for Allah." (Qur'an 57:22)

The Prophet (peace be upon him) told us that if we face any difficulties in life, we should not think that if only we had done something different, this wouldn't have happened to us, that the result would have been different. Instead we should remind ourselves that everything that happens, happens because Allah allowed it to happen, with His permission, and could not have happened any other way. This doesn't mean we cannot

learn from our experiences and try to do things differently in future, but we shouldn't dwell on and get too sad about things that have already happened.

"If a calamity befalls you, do not say, 'If only I had done that, it would have been like that.' Say instead, 'It is the destiny of Allah and He does whatever He wishes' for surely 'if' opens the door for Shai'tan." (Muslim)

Keeping things in perspective

However important the exam we are preparing for seems to us, however much we believe that the rest of our life depends on whether we pass or fail it, this isn't true. If we look at the lives of some of the most rich, successful and powerful people in the world, they failed many exams and many of them did not even complete their school education, let alone go to university.

We do not know what is written for us in the future. By failing this exam we might work even harder and do even better in the future than if we had passed it. By passing it, maybe we would have become arrogant and not worked as hard for our next, more important exam, and failed that. Also, the Prophet (peace be upon him) told us that everything that happens to a Muslim is good for him, if he faces difficulty he has

patience, and if he faces ease he is grateful, and both of these things bring us closer to Allah. Allah tells us in the Qur'an that after every hardship there is ease.

"...sometimes you may dislike something that is good for you, and sometimes you may like something that is bad for you. Only Allah knows the whole truth, not you." (Quran 2:216)

"How wonderful is the affair of the believer, for his affairs are all good, and this applies to no one but the believer. If something good happens to him, he is thankful for it and that is good for him. If something bad happens to him, he bears it with patience and that is good for him." (Muslim)

"Whatever Allah has decreed for His believing slave is a blessing, even if that is in the form of withholding; it is a favour even if that is in the form of a trial; and the calamity decreed by Him is fair, even if it us painful." (Madaarij al-Saalikeen)

Indeed, every hardship is followed by ease, indeed, every hardship is followed by ease. (Qur'an 94:5-6)

This does not mean that we shouldn't prepare or work hard. A man once came to the Prophet (peace be upon him) with his camel and asked the Prophet whether he should tie up his camel to stop it from running away or rely on Allah. The Prophet (peace be upon him) told him to tie up his camel and rely on Allah. When the Prophet (peace be upon him) went to war, he prayed to Allah to give the Muslims victory and he wore two sets of armour.

A man said, "O Messenger of Allah, should I tie my camel and trust in Allah, or should I leave her untied and trust in Allah?" The Prophet (peace be upon him) said, "Tie her and trust in Allah." (Tirmidhi)

We cannot think that if Allah has written for us to pass, for us to be successful and rich, it will happen even if we don't do anything. If we don't work hard and fail all our exams, we will have found out that that is what was written for us. We have to act as if we are in control of what will happen, while knowing that really anything and everything happens only with the will of Allah.

The most important exam

A good way to ensure we do not get too stressed about exams is to constantly remind ourselves that in truth there is only one exam that we should be really scared of failing, and so work as hard as we can to make sure we pass. Allah tells us in the Qur'an that He created us to worship Him and that is the real purpose of our life in this world.

I created Jinn and human beings only to worship Me. (Qur'an 51:56)

If we use the time we have in this life to please Allah, we will have passed the test and on the Day of Judgement He will reward us with everlasting life in Paradise. But if we waste our time in this world and displease Allah, we will have failed the test and on the Day of Judgement He will punish us with eternity in Hell.

By the age, humans are at a loss, except the believers who were righteous, and encouraged each other to be truthful and patient. (Qur'an 103)

So even if we were to pass every exam we sit, we get our dream job, we become famous, a world expert in our field, or even if we become prime minister or president of a country, or even King or Queen of the whole world, if we don't pass the final test and on the Day of Judgement we get thrown into Hell, what have we achieved? Have we been successful? Even if we lived to be a 1,000 years old, and had a life where we didn't have to do any work, just had fun all the time, we could buy whatever we wanted, could go wherever we wanted, could do whatever we wanted, if at the end of all that we had to spend forever in Hell, was it worth it?

Those who deny Our signs and consider them beneath them, the gates of Heaven will not open for them, nor will they enter Paradise until a camel can pass through the eye of a needle; that is how We punish the sinners. They shall have a bed of Hell fire, and there will be a covering of fire above them; that is how We punish wrongdoers. (Qur'an 7:40-41)

Even if the disbelievers owned everything on Earth twice over and tried to ransom themselves with it from the punishment of Judgement Day, it would not be accepted from them; theirs will be a painful punishment. They will long to come out of the Fire but won't be able to do so; theirs will be a lasting punishment. (Qur'an 5:36-37)

This doesn't mean we give up on the world and just concentrate on worshipping Allah. If Allah has blessed us with the ability to excel at something (such as being a doctor, lawyer, teacher, taxi driver, librarian, cleaner), we should use those skills to do a good job, help people, earn Halal money and look after ourselves and our family, and give in charity. All of these things are counted as worship of Allah. But we should also always remember the real reason we are on this Earth, and the exam we have to pass. So even if we work hard and try our best but fail the exams we do in this life, it doesn't matter as long as we don't fail the exam that will decide where we spend the eternity of our hereafter.

By the human He made perfect; so inspired him to follow either its vice or virtue. Whoever purified himself succeeded, and whoever was immoral failed himself. (Qur'an 91:7-10)

Believers, be patient, encourage each other to be patient, be disciplined, and be mindful of Allah so that you are successful. (Qur'an 3:200)

The Prophet (peace be upon him) said: "The first action for which a servant of Allah will be held accountable on the Day of Resurrection will be his prayers. If they are in order, he will have prospered and succeeded. If they are lacking, he will have failed and lost..." (Tirmidhi)

Conclusion

Exams are a part of life for each and every one of us. We should work hard for them and try to do our best, but remember that even people we think of as very rich and successful have failed exams in their lifetime. But the one exam we should always remember, that we cannot afford to fail, is the reason why we were created. This was to worship Allah and earn His pleasure, so on the Day of Judgement He will reward us with an eternal life in Paradise – that is the ultimate success.

Questions

- What are the different methods by which we can reduce our stress regarding exams?
- If we fail an exam, could we have passed by preparing better, or working faster, and more carefully during the exam?
- How might passing an exam be bad for us, and failing an exam be good for us?
- What is the most important exam we all face?
- What will the results of that exam determine?

Activities

- Do some research regarding someone very rich and powerful, find out about things that did not work out in their lives and what effect this had on them
- When you are preparing for your next exam, make sure you don't think you are too busy or the exam is too important for you to have time to remember Allah
- When you are preparing for your next exam, pray to Allah to give you whatever result is best for you, which only He knows, whether that is to pass or fail, and to give you patience and the ability to be thankful, whatever the result
- Every day, before you go to sleep, think about what preparation you did today for the most important exam – if you were to have to sit that exam today, think about whether you would pass or fail

4.6

Anxiety, Depression, Self-Harm and Suicide

Objectives

- To understand what someone suffering from depression and anxiety is experiencing
- To explore the different ways Islam teaches us to cope with depression and anxiety
- To consider why people self-harm and commit suicide, and the effects of this on themselves and their families

Keywords

- Anxiety
- Depression
- Self-harm
- Suicide

What is depression?

Sometimes people, including children, feel depressed and anxious. Some people think feeling depressed just means feeling sad, but it isn't. We all feel sad at times, maybe if we watch a sad movie or hear sad news, but this doesn't make us depressed.

Depression is a much deeper kind of sadness that seems like it will never go away. When you are depressed nothing is fun anymore, not even the things you used to enjoy. You feel like there is nothing to look forward to. You feel like you are worthless, that you will never achieve anything. You feel like you are a burden on those around you, that no-one would want to spend time with you. You might feel like crying all the time or even wish that you were dead. Sometimes people stop eating or being able to sleep properly, or might eat or sleep too much.

Sometimes something happens which causes us to become depressed, such as the death of a loved one, getting bullied at school or abused at home. But sometimes people feel depressed without anything significant happening. People who don't understand might say things like, "You've got nothing to be sad about," or, "You should be grateful for all the things you have." What they don't understand is that is that someone doesn't choose to be depressed, and once you are depressed you can't just choose to stop being depressed and be happy instead. And suffering from depression does not mean you are not grateful to Allah for all that He has blessed you with.

What is anxiety?

In the same way, anxiety is not just feeling worried. We all feel worried, afraid, or begin to panic in certain situations, such as before an exam or interview, or if we get into an argument or physical altercation. These are situations in which our mind and body needs to be alert and active, ready for action, so our heart beats faster, our pupils dilate, we start to sweat, our skin feels cold (especially our hands and feet), our mouth gets dry, we get butterflies in our tummy, and we lose our appetite. Normally, after the thing we were worried about is over, we calm down and feel better, more relaxed.

But people who suffer from anxiety might start to feel this way about things which shouldn't cause them to become anxious (such as whenever they have to go to school or work, or talk to someone). Or even after a stressful situation is over they can't stop feeling anxious. Or whenever they face a stressful situation they get so anxious that it stops them from being able to do anything at all. They might feel like they are

not good enough to accomplish anything, that it is impossible for them to be successful at even simple, everyday things. Suffering from anxiety can affect your sleep and eating, similar to depression. In fact, people often suffer from both anxiety and depression at the same time.

Self-harm and suicide

People who suffer from depression or anxiety sometimes hurt themselves (called self-harming). This can be by cutting their skin (often on their arms or legs, where the scars can be covered by clothes), or sometimes by burning (for example, using cigarettes or matches). They do this to cause themselves physical pain as a way of coping with the emotional and psychological difficulties they are going through. They are not in control of this but they are in control of the physical pain they are causing themselves, which can help them ignore the emotional and psychological pain for a short while.

When they cause themselves physical pain this also causes their brain to release a chemical called endorphins that makes them feel happy for a short while. But this can become addictive because once the endorphins run out, and the physical pain fades, it leaves them with the same psychological and emotional pain. But now they also have the added feeling of guilt and shame of having hurt themselves, the permanent scars they have left on their skin, and having to hide them from family and friends. People who self-harm in this way find it difficult to stop once they have established a habit, especially if nothing is being

being done to reduce the anxiety or depression they are suffering from.

Sometimes people who are suffering from anxiety or depression feel like their life is unbearable, that they cannot cope anymore and it would be better if they were dead, and commit suicide. However, suicide attempts (such as taking an overdose, shooting yourself or jumping off a building) are often unsuccessful and can lead to significant disabilities (e.g. paralysis, blindness, liver failure) for which lifelong medical care is required. Even if successful, they leave behind grieving loved ones who are often left with long-lasting feelings of guilt that the suicide was their fault and their failing in recognising the signs that things had gotten so bad.

Is self-harm and suicide allowed in Islam?

Self-harm and suicide are both not allowed in Islam, under any circumstance. Our bodies and our lives are a gift from Allah, our Lord and Creator. They are His to do whatever He wants to, whenever He wants, in whatever way He wants, and in the end, to take back at a time of His choosing. We have been forbidden from unnecessarily hurting our bodies and from taking our own lives. By doing so we are being extremely ungrateful to Allah.

The Prophet (peace be upon him) told us that a person who hurries his own death (by committing suicide) is forbidden from entering Paradise, and the way they kill themselves will be the way they are punished for eternity in Hell.

...and do not kill yourselves. Allah is Most Merciful to you. (Qur'an 4:29)

The Prophet (peace be upon him) said: "And whoever commits suicide with piece of iron will be punished with the same piece of iron in the Hell-Fire." (Bukhari)

The Prophet (peace be upon him) said: "A man was inflicted with wounds and he committed suicide, and so Allah said: 'My slave has caused death on himself hurriedly, so I forbid Paradise for him.'" (Bukhari)

Remembering that life is a test

The things that happen to us in this life only happen by the will of Allah. They are a test for us. At times in our lives this test will involve peace and ease, Allah is checking to see if we remember and are grateful to Him. At other times it will involve difficulty and hardship, Allah is checking to see if we are patient and turn back to Him, or alternatively if we complain and lose hope and faith.

"You will certainly be tested through your wealth and persons..." (Qur'an 3:186)

"We will certainly test you: with fear, hunger, loss of wealth, health and harvests..." (Qur'an 2:155)

...don't despair of Allah's kindness, it is only the disbelievers who despair of Allah's kindness. (Qur'an 12:87)

People suffering from anxiety and depression are going through a very difficult test. It might seem like it will never end and it is more than you can bear. But Allah knows each and every one of us, He knows what we are capable of even better than we know ourselves.

We created man, and know exactly what his desires urge him to do; in fact, We are nearer to him than his jugular vein. (Qur'an 50:16)

Allah tells us that He never places a burden on anyone more than they can bear, and He also tells us that after every hardship there is ease.

Allah does not burden anyone beyond their capacity... (Qur'an 2:286)

Indeed, every hardship is followed by ease, indeed, every hardship is followed by ease. (Qur'an 94:5-6)

He tells us that if we remember Him, if we are mindful of Him, then He give us a way out of every difficulty in ways we cannot even imagine, and that Allah is enough for anyone who puts their trust in Him.

...Whoever is mindful of Allah, He shall make a way out for him, and provide him sustenance from where he wouldn't expect. Whoever puts trust in Allah is enough for him... (Qur'an 65:2-3)

...put your trust in Allah. Allah suffices as a protector. (Qur'an 4:81)

Allah tells the believer to seek His help through patience and prayer, and He comforts them that He is with the patient person, He loves them.

Believers, find strength through patience and prayer – Allah is with those who are patient. (Qur'an 2:153)

Therefore, in reality this test is a blessing in disguise. It teaches us to rely completely on Allah, to turn to Him fully. It is a way we can be forgiven for our sins and draw closer to Allah and become one of His friends (Awliyah-Allah). In fact, the Prophet (peace be upon him) told us that Allah gives the hardest tests to those who are closest to Him, to the Prophets, and after them the Awliyah-Allah, and after them the believers according to their level of (faith).

The Prophet was asked, "O Messenger of Allah (peace be upon him), which people are tested most severely?" The Prophet (peace be upon him) said, "They are the prophets, then the next best, then the next best. A man is tried according to his religion. If he is firm in his religion, then his trials will be more severe." (Tirmidhi)

What Islam teaches us about how to deal with anxiety and depression

So what should a Muslim do when suffering from anxiety and/ or depression? The first thing is to realise, to truly believe that this is a test from Allah and it will not last

forever. Allah has chosen to give us this test because He knows that with His help we can pass this test, that we can bear with it.

But this does not mean that we shouldn't go to a doctor, tell them the difficulties we are going through and comply with treatment, whether it is talking therapy or taking medication. The Prophet (peace be upon him) told us to use medicine.

The Prophet (peace be upon him) said: "Treat sickness, for Allah has not created any disease except He has also created the cure..." (Tirmidhi)

So we should seek medical help and engage with it wholeheartedly, believing that it can help us (positive thinking is very important). Medicine is a mercy from Allah, it is a Sabab (a means) for Him helping us through this difficult test.

Alongside this we must turn back to Allah, to remember Him even more than we used to. Allah tells us in the Qur'an that only by remembering Him can our hearts find peace.

...those who believe, their hearts ill find peace in Allah's remembrance. The fact is, hearts find peace in the remembrance of Allah! (Qur'an 13:28)

There is nothing else in this whole world, not money, or fame or power, not a big house or expensive car, nor a good job, a big family or lots of friends, there is nothing else that can bring true happiness except for the remembrance of Allah.

If we look at the life of the Prophet (peace be upon him), whatever he was doing he was also engaged in the constant remembrance of Allah. He has taught us so many different ways, so find one that helps you, that makes you feel calm

Maybe it will be in reading the Qur'an, with its translation if you do not understand the Arabic. Reciting Surah Fatiha can help cure not only spiritual diseases but also ones of the body and mind, for this reason it is called 'the cure' as per a Hadith from Bukhari. Maybe it is listening to beautiful recitations of the Qur'an:

...the Qur'an is a healing and kindness for believers... (Qur'an 17:82)

Maybe it is reading extra Nawafil after Salah. Maybe it is spending more time in the Mosque. Maybe it is attending Islamic lectures. Maybe it is doing a Tasbih of a specific Adhkar (remembrance of Allah):

The Prophet (peace be upon him) said: "If anyone constantly seeks pardon (from Allah), Allah will appoint for him a way out of every distress and a relief from every anxiety, and will provide sustenance for him from where he expects not." (Abu Dawood)

Maybe it is reciting more peace and blessings upon the Prophet:

Syedina Ubayy ibn Ka'b (may Allah be pleased with him) said: "O Messenger of Allah, I send a great deal of blessings upon you; how much of my Dua should be sending blessings upon you? The Prophet replied: "Whatever you wish." I said: "One quarter?" He said: "Whatever you wish, and if you do more, that will be better for you." I said: "One half?" He said: "Whatever you wish and if you do more, that will be better for you." I said: "Two thirds?" He said: "Whatever you wish and if you do more, that will be better for you." I said: "I will make all of my Dua for you." He said: "Then your concerns will be taken care of and your sins will be forgiven." (Tirmidhi)

Maybe it is listening to Nasheeds. Maybe it is just doing Wudu, sitting on your prayer mat alone in your room, and talking to Allah, with the surety in your heart that He is listening to you, telling Him how you feel, telling Him how difficult you are finding life right now but that you still want to please Him, crying to Him, asking and begging Him for help. See for yourself the effect this has; how peaceful you will feel afterwards.

Your Lord said: "Call on Me and I shall answer you." (Qur'an 40:60)

Avoid following the advice of Shaitan

In any battle we must recognise our enemy and their intentions. Allah tells us in the Qur'an that Shaitan is our enemy.

...don't let Satan, the arch-deceiver, draw you away from Allah. Satan is your enemy, treat him as such. He invites his followers to become companions of the fiery Blaze. (Qur'an 35:5-6)

He wants us to fail these tests, to go through difficulties and hardship but not gain any benefit from then. So he makes us feel like we cannot cope, he makes us feel angry with Allah, he encourages us to say things like, "Why is Allah punishing me, what have I done to deserve it?" or that, "Allah has forgotten me!", and to do Haram things like self-harm and commit suicide. He tricks us, lies to us that these things will help, but they don't, they only make things worse.

...Whoever takes Satan as a protector rather than Allah will become a clear loser. He promises them and gives them hopes, but Satan's promises are mere deception. (Qur'an 4:120)

The Prophet (peace be upon him) taught us that we should not even pray for death, let alone take our own life. He taught us to pray instead, "O Allah! Keep me alive as long as life is better for me, and let me die if death is better for me." (Bukhari)

Noticing the signs and helping others

We may not suffer from depression or anxiety but start to notice signs in our family or friends. They might not be smiling or talking as much as

as they used to. When they smile, you might notice they are doing it with their mouths but not their eyes, you can tell it is a fake smile so people won't know how they are really feeling inside. They might not want to eat the things they used to enjoy, or go out with friends. They might seem to be rude, ignoring you when you try talking to them, or not answering phone calls, or getting angry with you for little things.

If you notice these things do your best to help them. Ask them how they are, ask them what is wrong, tell them what you have noticed in their behaviour and that you want to help them. Try and spend more time with them (even if they say they don't want to spend time with you), to talk to and listen to what they have to say, to be a shoulder for them to cry on. We should also remember these people in our prayers, to ask Allah to heal them.

The Prophet (peace be upon him) said: "Whoever relieves the hardship of a believer in this world, Allah will relieve his hardship on the Day of Resurrection. Whoever helps ease one in difficulty, Allah will make it easy for him in this world and in the Hereafter...Allah helps the servant as long as he helps his brother..." (Muslim)

Conclusion

In the same way that our body can become ill, so can our minds, and two of these illnesses that many people, even children suffer from are depression and anxiety. As Muslims we believe that illnesses are a test from Allah, to see whether we will remember Him, rely upon Him, and be patient until He cures us. People suffering from anxiety and depression can sometimes resort to self-harm and even suicide but in Islam these are strictly forbidden; they are ways the Shaitan tries to trick us into failing the test. Instead, Islam teaches that during difficult times in our life we should remember Allah, pray to Him, cry to Him, and be patient, and by doing this He will forgive our sins, cure us, and bring us closer to Him.

Questions

- What is depression?
- What is anxiety?
- Why do people self-harm?
- Is self-harm or suicide allowed in Islam?
- How does Islam teach us to cope with depression and anxiety?
- How can these illnesses be blessings for us?
- What should be do if we start to notice signs of depression or anxiety in our friends or family?

Activities

- Do some research on how depression affects people's lives
- Do some research on how anxiety affects people's lives
- Think about a time in your life you felt sad about something, imagine how it would be if that feeling of sadness didn't end
- Think about a time in your life you felt anxious about something, imagine feeling like that about every little thing you have to do every day
- Try and spend some time every day, on your own, talking to Allah, thanking Him for everything He has given you and telling Him how you are feeling
- If there is anyone you know who you think might be suffering from anxiety or depression make an effort to spend time with them, talk to them, find out what is going on in their lives, try to help them through this difficult time and pray for them

Glossary

Ablution / Wudu – the act of washing ourselves or part of our body, a type of ritual purification

Adhan – the Islamic call to prayer

Ahl al-Bayt – people of the house, refers to family of the Prophet Muhammad (peace be upon him)

Al-Lawh al-Mahfuz – the Preserved Tablet, upon which is inscribed everything that has, and will ever happen

Awliyah Allah – friends of Allah, the saints

Barakat – blessings

Dawah – invitation to Islam

Fard – obligatory

Fiqh – Islamic jurisprudence, i.e., the science of deriving and understanding Shariah, or Islamic law

Fitra – a state of purity and innocence that all human beings are born with, our innate nature

Ghusl – a type of ritual purification that involves washing our whole body

Hadith – a record of the words or actions of the Prophet Muhammad (peace be upon him)

Hadith Kudsi – a Hadith in which the content is directly revealed by Allah, but the wording is attributed to the Prophet Muhammad (peace be upon him)

Hajj / Umrah – the greater and lesser pilgrimage to Makkah, one of the five pillars of Islam

Halal – permissible

Haram – impermissible

Hijab – a religious veil worn by women, usually covering the head and chest

Hafiz / Hafiza / Huffaz – the masculine, feminine and plural form of the word denoting someone who has memorised the entire Qur'an

Ihsan – beautification, perfection, or excellence

Istighfar – repentance, seeking forgiveness

Jihad – to struggle or strive

Jinn – the only other creation of Allah other than humans to have free will. They were created from a smokeless fire, and are invisible to humans but can appear in different forms

Madhab – a school of religious law

Mus'haf – the written form of the Qur'an

Nafs – has been defined in various ways, including the self, the soul, the ego, the psyche

Nawafil – voluntary or supererogatory acts of worship

Qadr – predestination, the Divine will

Rak'at – a single unit of prayer in the Salah

Riba – usury / interest, or any other form of exploitation or unjust gain made in trade or business

Sadaqa / Zakat – voluntary and obligatory charity, one of the five pillars of Islam

Salah – ritual prayers performed by Muslims while facing the direction of the Ka'ba, alone or in congregation, including the five obligatory daily prayers which are one of the five pillars of Islam

Sawm – fasting, obligatory within the month of Ramadan, or voluntary fasting at any other time of the year, one of the five pillars of Islam

Shai'tan/Iblis – Satan / the devil, a Jinn who lived with the Angels in the Heavens prior to disobeying Allah

Shariah – Islamic law

Siratul Mustaqim – the straight path, the middle way (i.e., in between extremes)

Sunnah – traditions and practices of the Prophet Muhammad (peace be upon him) which provide a model for how Muslims should live their lives

Syedina / Syedatuna – masculine and feminine form of a term used as a title or out of respect, meaning 'our leader' or 'our master'

Taqwa – consciousness of Allah that stops us from disobeying Him in fear of His anger and punishment

Tassawuf / Sufism – the facet of Islam concerned with purification of the inner and outer self

Tawakkul – trust / reliance in Allah

Ummah – a people, community or nation, used in the Qur'an to denote the people to whom Allah sends a Prophet (peace be upon them all)

Zina – fornication or adultery